Focus on LITERACY

Teacher's Resource Book 3

Barry and Anita Scholes

COLLINS

Authors: Barry and Anita Scholes

Design: Grasshopper Design Company

Editor: James Ryan

Cover image: Olney Vasan, Tony Stone Images

Illustrations: Bethan Matthews

Published by Collins Educational
An imprint of HarperCollins*Publishers* Ltd
77–85 Fulham Palace Road
Hammersmith
London W6 8JB

Telephone ordering and information:
0870 0100 441

The HarperCollins website address is:
www.**fire**and**water**.com

First published 1999

Reprinted 2000

Text © Barry and Anita Scholes 1999
Design and illustrations © HarperCollins*Publishers* Ltd 1999

Sources
Unit 30: *Fred and the Angel* by Martin Waddell (Walker, 1989).

Every effort has been made to trace copyright holders and to obtain their permission for the use of copyright material. The author and publishers will gladly receive any information enabling them to rectify any error or omission in subsequent editions.

Barry and Anita Scholes assert the moral right to be identified as the authors of this work.

All rights reserved. Any educational institution that has purchased one copy of this book may make duplicate copies of pages identified as copiable for use exclusively within that institution. (Copiable pages can be identified by the copyright notice printed at the bottom of the page.) No other part of this publication may be reproduced, stored in a retrieval system or transmitted in any form or by any means – electronic, mechanical, photocopying, recording or otherwise – without either the prior written permission of the Publisher or a licence permitting restricted copying in the United Kingdom issued by the Copyright Licensing Agency Ltd, 90 Tottenham Court Road, London W1P 0LP.

ISBN 0 00 302519 5

British Library Cataloguing in Publication Data
A catalogue record for this book is available from the British Library.

Printed in Great Britain by Martins the Printers, Berwick-upon-Tweed

Contents

Focus on Literacy and the National Literacy Strategy — 4

The course components — 8
Big Book contents — 8
Pupil's Book contents — 11
Homework Book contents — 14
Copymaster checklist — 15

Teacher's notes — 17

Term 1 — 18
Half-termly planner — 18
Teacher's notes — 20

Term 2 — 40
Half-termly planner — 40
Teacher's notes — 42

Term 3 — 62
Half-termly planner — 62
Teacher's notes — 64

Copymasters — 85
Copymasters 1–30 — 86
Award certificates — 116
Record sheets — 117

Appendices — 123
NLS and *Focus on Literacy*: overview charts — 124
High frequency word list — 127

Focus on Literacy and the National Literacy Strategy

You will find in *Focus on Literacy* a strong support in the teaching of reading and writing within the context of a literacy hour. All the literacy objectives of the National Literary Strategy for each term may be covered by using the Big Book anthologies together with the Pupil's Book, the Homework Book, the Copymasters and the Teacher's Resource Book. Here, in one grand design, are sufficient teaching materials for five full literacy hours per week throughout the entire school year.

The aims of *Focus on Literacy*

The aims of *Focus on Literacy* are identical to those of the National Literacy Strategy: to develop each child's ability to read and write. It promotes their development by honing the literary skills necessary to meet the Range, Key Skills, and Standard English and Language Study of the National Curriculum Programmes of Study.

These skills are wide-ranging and specific, and worthy of review:

- to read and write with confidence, fluency and understanding
- to use a full range of reading cues (phonic, graphic, syntactic, contextual) to self-monitor their reading and correct their own mistakes
- to understand the sound and spelling system and use this to read and spell accurately
- to acquire fluent and legible handwriting
- to have an interest in words and word meanings, and to increase vocabulary
- to know, understand and be able to write in a range of genres in fiction and poetry, and understand and be familiar with some of the ways that narratives are structured through basic literary ideas of setting, character and plot
- to understand and be able to use a range of non-fiction texts
- to plan, draft, revise and edit their own writing
- to have a suitable technical vocabulary through which they can understand and discuss their reading and writing
- to be interested in books, read with enjoyment and evaluate and justify preferences
- to develop their powers of imagination, inventiveness and critical awareness through reading and writing.

The NLS framework and *Focus on Literacy*

The NLS teaching objectives for reading and writing are set out in termly units to ensure progression. Each term's work focuses on specific reading genres and related writing activities. *Focus on Literacy* offers carefully selected examples of these reading genres and stimulating activities relating to them.

The overall structure is the same for each term and is divided into three strands: text, sentence and word levels. Text level refers to comprehension and composition, sentence level to grammar and punctuation and word level to phonics, spelling and vocabulary. The activities in *Focus on Literacy* offer many opportunities for the development of handwriting, while leaving you free to follow your school's own writing policy.

The Literacy Hour and *Focus on Literacy*

The NLS framework requires a literacy hour as part of school work each day. The literacy hour is designed to establish a common pattern for all classes and is carefully structured to ensure a balance between whole class and group teaching, as the diagram below shows.

4 *KS1 and KS2*
Reviewing, reflecting, consolidating teaching points, and presenting work covered in the lesson.

1 *KS1 and KS2*
Shared text work (a balance of reading and writing).

Whole class approx **10** mins

Whole class approx **15** mins

Group and independent work approx **20** mins

Whole class approx **15** mins

3 *KS1*
Independent reading, writing or word work, while the teacher works with at least two ability groups each day on guided text work (reading or writing).
KS2
Independent reading, writing or word and sentence work, while the teacher works with at least one ability group each day on guided text work (reading or writing).

2 *KS1*
Focused word work.
KS2
A balance over the term of focused word work or sentence work.

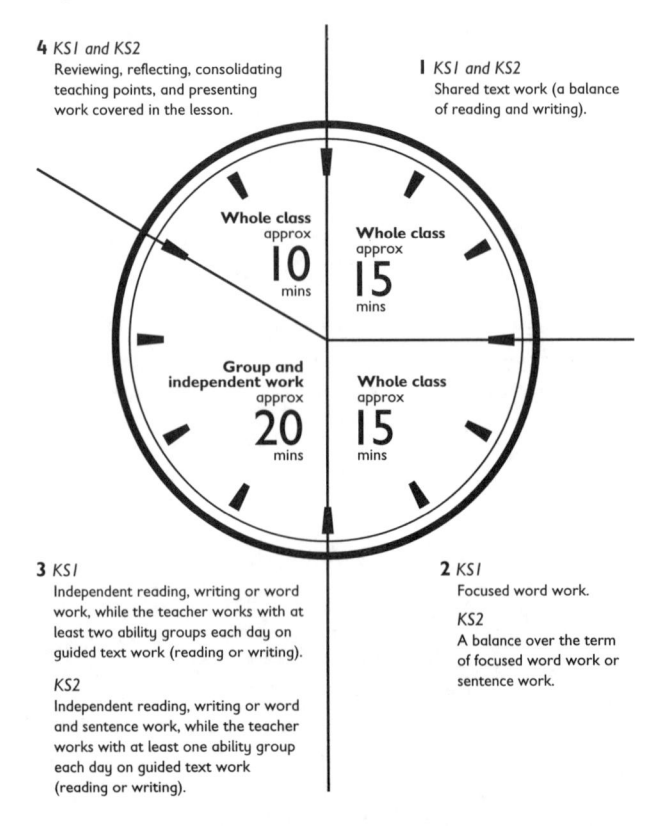

This structure enables you to spend up to 100 per cent of your time in direct teaching. Children work in a direct teaching relationship for approximately 60 per cent of the time and independently for the remaining 40 per cent.

The high-quality texts of *Focus on Literacy* and the related activities directly meet the NLS objectives, and so relieve you of the burden of deciding *what* to teach. The teacher's notes support you in planning *how* to use the materials in your teaching.

Shared whole class time
Shared whole class time takes place during the first half of the literacy hour. It is divided into 15 minutes of shared text work (a balance of reading and writing) and 15 minutes of focused word and sentence work. This is the time when you can effectively model the reading/writing process with the children.

In shared reading you can help to extend reading skills in line with the NLS objectives, teaching and reinforcing grammar, punctuation and vocabulary.

The reading texts also provide ideas and structures for shared writing. Working with the whole class, you create the opportunity to teach grammar and spelling skills, to demonstrate features of layout and presentation and to focus on editing and refining work. The shared writing will also be the starting point for independent writing.

Independent activities
The shared whole class time of the literary hour is followed by 20 minutes of independent activities. During this time you will probably work with a guided reading or writing group, while the children will be working independently, but within a group organised by ability to cater for differentiation.

To help you with this, the word and sentence work in the Pupil's Book is divided into two, three or four sections identified as A, B, C and D; A is the easiest and D is the hardest. It is important to match carefully these activities to the children's ability, and to explain them thoroughly before the children begin. This leaves you free to work with your group without interruptions from children seeking your further support.

Each section is short so that children will be able to complete the activities you select in the time available. The Homework Book is available for those who finish early and wish to keep busy, as well as for work outside the classroom. Other activities which the children may do during this time are independent reading and preparing presentations for the class.

It is suggested that you aim to work with each guided reading and writing group for two sessions per week, organised so that you see each child in the class at least once.

Plenary
The final 10 minutes of the literacy hour is a plenary session for reviewing, reflecting upon and consolidating teaching points, and presenting work covered in the lesson. This is an essential element of the hour. It is important to plan this activity so that every child has the opportunity to feed back once as part of their group during the course of a week. A different objective will be featured each day so that each objective is reinforced in turn. This will allow you to monitor each group's progress and highlight the teaching/learning points as necessary.

Using *Focus On Literacy*

The Big Book anthologies
There are three Big Book anthologies, each covering a term's work. These consist of carefully chosen texts for shared work on word, sentence and text levels. The extracts also provide the context for the independent activities. Each unit provides texts for a week's shared reading.

Each extract in the anthology begins with a short introduction, placing the text that follows in context. The extract is accompanied by a *To think and talk about* section to prompt and stimulate the children's responses.

Further teaching points and suggestions are given in the Teacher's Resource Book.

The Pupil's Book
The Pupil's Book is made up of 30 units. Each unit begins with the main text and is followed by the independent activities for the week.

To help you with differentiation, the independent activities are identified for level of difficulty, section A being the easiest and D the hardest. Each section is scaled to a workable size. By matching the level of difficulty to a group's ability level, you can help assure that children can complete the activities in the time available.

The five-day spread
The independent activity for **Day 1** is text-based. Section A has questions for literal recall, while those in section B are inferential. These independent questions are in addition to those in the *To think and talk about* section, which are intended as shared reading questions in order for you to help the children to explore the text at greater depth.

Day 2 independent activities focus on word, sentence or text work.

Day 3 begins with shared writing, followed by independent writing.

Day 4 is the same as Day 3.

Day 5 completes the word, sentence or text work.

"Stickers" provide the children with the facts they need to complete the work and make the most of the activities.

The Homework Book

The Homework Book contains activities which consolidate and extend the work in the Pupil's Book. This book is equally useful in the classroom outside the literacy hour and out of the classroom for work at home.

The Teacher's Resource Book

The Teacher's Resource Book comprises notes, copymasters, assessment masters, record sheets and NLS charts. It also outlines a basic approach to each unit in the Big Books and Pupil's Book and includes two award certificates.

The teacher's notes and you

The teacher's notes help you use the *Focus on Literacy* material to the best advantage. The notes are arranged in five sections, each covering one literacy hour. These are further subdivided according to the literacy format: shared text/shared writing work, focused word/sentence work, independent work, and plenary.

A termly planning chart introduces each group of ten units. This chart lists the range of texts for that term, the word, sentence and text work which is explicitly covered, and the continuous work which will be part of your teaching throughout the term, such as practising reading and spelling strategies.

The teacher's notes for each text are organised to facilitate the literacy hour.

A *Key Learning Objectives* box lists the key literacy objectives covered in that week's work and a *Resources* box identifies the range of texts covered, details of the extracts, and the page references of all the components used in the unit.

Details are given of any special preparation you need to do for the unit, for example providing dictionaries.

The *Shared reading* section lists teaching points and suggestions on how to explore the meaning of the text, in line with the literacy framework objectives. In fiction and poetry this entails exploring genres, settings, characters, plots, themes, figurative language, authorship and the way different texts are organised. In non-fiction text this involves genres, structures and presentation, identifying main points, skimming and scanning, following an argument, exploring steps in a process, comparing different sources and differentiating fact, opinion and persuasion.

The texts often provide both structure and content for writing activities, and the context for many of the activities at sentence and word level on the Copymasters.

The *Shared writing* section offers guidance on how texts are composed. The main text studied in earlier shared reading sessions will provide the ideas and structure for this writing. Each shared writing activity is the starting point for subsequent independent writing.

The *Focused sentence/word work* section offers appropriate teaching points and suggestions for investigating text in detail to explore how its message is influenced by style: language, grammar, choice of vocabulary and presentation. The Pupil's Book supports independent consolidation of the work.

The *Independent work* section introduces the independent reading, writing or word and sentence activities which may be found in the Pupil's Book, the Homework Book or on Copymasters.

The *Plenary* section has suggestions for reviewing and reflecting upon the work covered, consolidating teaching points and presenting work.

A *Consolidation and extension* section has ideas and suggestions for follow-up activities.

The *Homework* section describes the related activity in the Homework Book.

Copymasters

The Copymasters offer a range of support material among which are book reviews, planning sheets, charts for collecting and classifying words, consolidation and extension work.

Assessment

To facilitate assessment there is an assessment master for each term, and a self-assessment master for the year's work.

Record keeping

Record sheets are provided at the back of the Teacher's Resource Book. They feature a summary of the term's objectives, each with a space for your comments.

Award certificate

Photocopiable award certificates are provided to reward significant individual achievements in literacy.

NLS charts

A chart listing all literacy objectives for the year, and showing how these are covered by *Focus on Literacy* materials, is included in the back of the Teacher's Resource Book.

Basic approach to each unit

The basic approach to each unit in *Focus on Literacy* is as follows:

Day 1

Shared **reading** of the week's main text in the Big Book.

Focused word/sentence work based on the main text.

Independent text work on the main text, which is reproduced in the Pupil's Book.

Plenary session for which there are suggestions in the teacher's notes.

Day 2

Further shared **reading** of the main text.

Further focused word/sentence work based on the main text.

Independent word, sentence or text work in the Pupil's Book.

Plenary suggestions in the teacher's notes.

Day 3

Shared **writing**, using the main text as a model or stimulus.

Focused word/sentence work, appropriate to the shared writing task.

Independent writing, using guidance in the Pupil's Book.

Plenary suggestions in the teacher's notes.

Day 4

Shared **reading** of the second text in the Big Book.

Focused word/sentence work based on the second text.

Continuation of the independent writing from Day 3.

Plenary suggestions in the teacher's notes.

Day 5

Further shared **reading** of the second text.

Focused word/sentence work based on the second text.

Independent word, sentence or text work in the Pupil's Book.

Plenary suggestions in the teacher's notes.

This approach is flexible, occasionally varied to make the most of the week's activities. For example, the shared reading for Day 4 might be replaced by shared writing when more extended written work is being developed; shared writing might begin on Day 2; or the second text might be shared on Day 2.

Work outside the literacy hour

The Copymasters and Homework Book provide activities for outside the literacy hour and outside the classroom.

The extracts in *Focus on Literacy* are only part of the genre coverage. You will need time outside of the literacy hour to read aloud to your class, giving children the opportunity to hear complete stories, novels and poems. You will also need to show them complete non-fiction texts, so that features such as covers, blurbs, information about authors, contents, indexes and chapter headings can be discussed and appreciated. Children will need further time for their own independent reading for interest and pleasure, and older pupils will need time for extended writing.

You can help to reinforce genre features when children choose books for independent reading, or during guided reading sessions when you are working with a group.

THE COURSE COMPONENTS

Big Book contents

BIG BOOK 3A   TERM 1

Unit	Pages	
1	4–5	Charlie and Ben Move House from *The Moving Mystery*, Carmen Harris
	6–7	Removal Day from *The Moving Mystery*, Carmen Harris
2	8–9	An Exciting Letter from *Philomena Hall and the Best Kept Gerbil Competition*, Roy Apps
	10–11	The Postbox Mystery from *The Postbox Mystery*, Robert Swindells
3	12–15	The School Bell from *The School Bell*, Jacquie Buttriss and Ann Callander
	16–17	Breakfast at Seaview from *No Entry – Two Short Plays for Seven to Eight Parts*, Jan Carew
4	18–21	A Cage for a Mouse from *The Trouble with Mice*, Pat Moon
	22–23	The Mouse Escapes from *The Trouble with Mice*, Pat Moon
5	24–25	Walking the Goldfish from *Walking the Goldfish*, Michael Hardcastle
	26–27	Setting up an Aquarium
6	28–29	The Senses *Jigsaw Puddle*, Emily Hearn; *Ice Cream and Fizzy Lemonade*, Stanley Cook; *Sounds*, Alexander Kennedy; *Smells*, A. Elliott-Cannon
	30–31	Sight and Touch *The Feel of Things*, A. Elliott-Cannon; *What is Red?*, Mary O'Neill
7	32–34	Diwali from *Diwali*, Kerena Marchant
	35	Using a Contents Page from *High Days and Holidays*, David Self
8	36–37	The Flat Man from *The Flat Man*, Rose Impey
	38–39	I Can't Get to Sleep *I Can't Get to Sleep*, Richard Burns
9	40–41	Nesting Birds from *The Nature Trail Book of Birdwatching*, Usborne
	42–43	Bird Spotting
10	44–47	Shape Poems *one*, e.e. cummings; *Snake*, Keith Bosley; *Sky Day Dream*, Robert Froman; *Mosquito*, Marie Zbierski; *O my!*, Anon
	48	Whoosh! *Whoosh!*, Max Fatchen

BIG BOOK 3B   TERM 2

Unit	Pages	
11	4–7	Fables The Foolish Crow The Greedy Dog from *Aesop's Fables*, retold by Anne Gatti The Sparrow and the Ostrich The Persistent Dog from *Fables from Africa*, retold by Jan Knappert
	8–9	The Lion's Share from *Fables from Africa*, retold by Jan Knappert
12	10–11	Wolf Tales The Rabbit and the Wolf from *Turkish Folk-tales*, retold by Barbara K. Walker
	12–13	The Three Little Pigs from *The Three Little Pigs*, Joseph Jacobs
13	14–16	Polly and the Wolf from *Clever Polly and the Stupid Wolf*, Catherine Storr
	17–19	The Spell from *Tales of Polly and the Hungry Wolf*, Catherine Storr
14	20–21	The Birth of the Sun from *Creation Stories*, retold by Maureen Stewart
	22–23	The First People from *Beginnings*, ed. P. Farmer
15	24–25	Instructions Chocolate Coconut Balls from *Divali*, Howard Marsh
	26	Vanishing Colours
	27	A Plan of a Classroom
16	28–29	Games Achi and Nine Men's Morris
	30–31	Playground Chants and Rhymes *Skipping Rope Song*, Dionne Brand; *School Dinners*, Anon
17	32–33	The Meaning of Words from *Collins Primary Dictionary* and *Collins Junior Thesaurus*
	34–35	Spellings and Meanings from *Collins Independent Dictionary*, Ginny Lapage
18	36–37	Rats! from *The Pied Piper of Hamelin*, Rose Impey
	38–39	The Pied Piper from *The Pied Piper of Hamelin*, Robert Browning
19	40–41	Odysseus and Polyphemus from *The One-eyed Giant and Other Monsters from the Greek Myths*, Anne Rockwell
	42–43	Heracles
20	44–45	The Spell-Hound from *The Saga of Erik the Viking*, Terry Jones
	46–48	The Spell-Hound Speaks from *The Saga of Erik the Viking*, Terry Jones

BIG BOOK CONTENTS

BIG BOOK 3C — TERM 3

Unit	Pages	
21	4–5	Alphabetic Lists An index, from *Let's Look at Big Cats*, Rhoda Nottridge A Telephone Directory
	6–7	Yellow Pages
22	8–10	Word Play *Rules*, Karla Kuskin; *Whipper-snapper*, Willard R. Espy; *Recipe for a Hippopotamus Sandwich*, Shel Silverstein; *Teacher said …*, Judith Nicholls
	11	On the Ning Nang Nong *On the Ning Nang Nong*, Spike Milligan
23	12–13	Hiding in the Dark from *Danny, the Champion of the World*, Roald Dahl
	14–15	A Marvellous Mixture from *George's Marvellous Medicine*, Roald Dahl
24	16–17	The Great Mouse Plot from *Boy*, Roald Dahl
	18–19	The Next Morning from *Boy*, Roald Dahl
25	20–21	A Snake in the Garden from *Jazeera in the Sun*, Lisa Bruce
	22–23	The Chase from *Skull Island*, Lesley Sims
26	24–27	The Library Fiction books Non-fiction books
	28–29	Food
27	30–32	Jacqueline Hyde from *Jacqueline Hyde*, Robert Swindells
	33–34	Looking for Fun from *Jacqueline Hyde*, Robert Swindells
28	35–37	A Sudden Glow of Gold from *A Sudden Glow of Gold*, Anne Fine
	38–39	Old Harwick Hall from *Step by Wicked Step*, Anne Fine
29	40–42	Word Puzzles *Strange but True*, Anon; *Wild Flowers*, Peter Newell
	43	More Word Puzzles *Riddle*, Judith Nicholls; *UR 2 GOOD*, Michael Rosen
30	44–48	Letters

THE COURSE COMPONENTS

Pupil's Book contents

TERM 1

Unit 1	p. 2	From *The Moving Mystery*, Carmen Harris
	p. 3	Comprehension; writing sentences
	p. 4	Writing a description (setting); questions and question marks

Unit 2	p. 5	From *Philomena Hall and the Best Kept Gerbil Competition*, Roy Apps
	p. 6	Comprehension; speech marks; words ending in *-le*
	p. 7	Writing a description (setting); words ending in *-ing*

Unit 3	p. 8	From *The School Bell*, Jacquie Buttriss and Ann Callander
	p. 9	Comprehension; exclamation marks; different kinds of sentences
	p. 10	Writing a playscript; different kinds of sentences

Unit 4	p. 11	From *The Trouble with Mice*, Pat Moon
	p. 12	Comprehension; verbs; verbs for ways of speaking
	p. 13	Writing a conversation as a playscript; prefixes: *dis-*, *un-*

Unit 5	p. 14	From *Walking the Goldfish*, Michael Hardcastle
	p. 15	Comprehension; more about verbs: synonyms, opposites; cloze
	p. 16	Non-chronological writing; captioned picture story
	p. 17	Setting up an aquarium; verbs: past and present tenses

Unit 6	p. 18	Poems on the senses
	p. 19	Comprehension; synonyms
	p. 20	Writing a list poem; poems on the senses
	p. 21	Adjectives

Unit 7	p. 22	From *Diwali*, Kerena Marchant
	p. 23	Comprehension; synonyms for the high-frequency words *got* and *nice*; spelling by analogy with known words, *-ight*
	p. 24	Non-chronological writing; using a contents page

Unit 8	p. 25	From *The Flat Man*, Rose Impey
	p. 26	Comprehension; verbs: past and present tenses
	p. 27	Writing a story in paragraphs; prefixes: *pre-*, *de-*, *re-*

Unit 9	p. 28	From *The Nature Trail Book of Birdwatching*, Usborne
	p. 29	Comprehension; presenting information as a chart
	p. 30	Drawing a diagram; context clues to meaning; making notes using key words
	p. 31	Bird spotting; presenting information as a chart

Unit 10	p. 32	Shape poems
	p. 33	Calligrams; using a thesaurus; calligram sentences
	p. 34	Writing shape poems; calligram sentences

PUPIL'S BOOK CONTENTS

TERM 2

Unit 11	p. 35	Fables
	p. 36	Comprehension; plurals: *-es*; suffixes: *-er*, *-est*
	p. 37	Writing a fable; suffix: *-y*
Unit 12	p. 38	From *Turkish Folk-tales*, retold by Barbara K. Walker
	p. 39	Sequencing key incidents; *is* and *are*, *was* and *were*
	p. 40	Exploring character by writing a letter; verb agreement
Unit 13	p. 41	From *Clever Polly and the Stupid Wolf*, Catherine Storr
	p. 42	Sequencing key incidents; apostrophe in short forms; singular and plural
	p. 43	Writing a sequel; punctuation
Unit 14	p. 44	From *Creation Stories*, retold by Maureen Stewart
	p. 45	Sequencing key incidents; adjectives
	p. 46	Writing a creation myth; more about adjectives; opposites
Unit 15	p. 47	From *Divali*, Howard Marsh; making a rainbow disc
	p. 48	Making a flow chart; making notes; verbs in the first, second and third person
	p. 49	Writing instructions; writing a recipe; compound words
Unit 16	p. 50	Games
	p. 51	Comprehension; homophones: *to*, *too*, *two*; word fun: missing letters, word pairs
	p. 52	Writing rules for a board game; word fun: word step, anagrams, adding a letter to make a new word
Unit 17	p. 53	From *Collins Primary Dictionary* and *Collins Junior Thesaurus*
	p. 54	Using a dictionary and thesaurus; alphabetical order; synonyms
	p. 55	Using a dictionary; silent letters
Unit 18	p. 56	From *The Pied Piper of Hamelin*, Rose Impey
	p. 57	Sequencing key incidents; headlines; inferring meaning
	p. 58	Writing a sequel to *The Pied Piper*; opposites
Unit 19	p. 59	From *The One-eyed Giant and Other Monsters from the Greek Myths*, Anne Rockwell
	p. 60	Comprehension; suffixes: *-ness*, *-ful*, *-less*; plurals
	p. 61	Writing a sequel to 'Odysseus and Polyphemus'; collective nouns
Unit 20	p. 62	From *The Saga of Erik the Viking*, Terry Jones
	p. 63	Comprehension; using a thesaurus
	p. 64	Writing a letter; continuing the story; designing a poster; grammatical agreement

PUPIL'S BOOK CONTENTS

TERM 3

Unit 21   p. 65   From *Let's Look at Big Cats*, Rhoda Nottridge
            p. 66   Using an index; alphabetical order; using a dictionary
            p. 67   Writing alphabetically ordered texts; using an index

Unit 22   p. 68   Word play poems
            p. 69   Comprehension; synonyms; rhymes
            p. 70   Writing poems from models; *On the Ning Nang Nong*, Spike Milligan
            p. 71   Alliteration; prefixes: *non-*, *mis-*, *anti-*, *co-*

Unit 23   p. 72   From *Danny, the Champion of the World*, Roald Dahl
            p. 73   Comprehension; pronouns
            p. 74   Writing a story linked to reading; first, second and third person pronouns

Unit 24   p. 75   From *Boy*, Roald Dahl
            p. 76   Comprehension; speech marks; using conjunctions: *when*, *while*, *since*
            p. 77   Writing an extended story

Unit 25   p. 78   From *Jazeera in the Sun*, Lisa Bruce
            p. 79   Comprehension; personal and possessive pronouns
            p. 80   Writing a character's own account of an incident in a story; homonyms

Unit 26   p. 81   Library classification
            p. 82   Sorting fiction books; making notes
            p. 83   Making your own information book

Unit 27   p. 84   From *Jacqueline Hyde*, Robert Swindells
            p. 85   Cloze procedure; compound words; homonyms
            p. 86   From *Jacqueline Hyde*, Robert Swindells; writing a story linked to reading
            p. 87   Using conjunctions: *so*, *if*, *though*

Unit 28   p. 88   From *A Sudden Glow of Gold*, Anne Fine
            p. 89   Comprehension; cloze procedure; words which signal time
            p. 90   Plotting episodes modelled on a known story; apostrophe in short forms

Unit 29   p. 91   Word puzzles
            p. 92   Comprehension; homonyms; crossword
            p. 93   Writing word puzzles: crossword, puns, riddles; homonyms; writing a tongue-twister

Unit 30   p. 94   Letters
            p. 95   Comprehension; first, second and third person
            p. 96   Writing letters

THE COURSE COMPONENTS

Homework Book contents

TERM 1

Unit 1	p. 2	Capital letters, full stops and question marks
Unit 2	p. 3	Speech marks
Unit 3	p. 4	Different kinds of sentences
Unit 4	p. 5	Verbs for ways of speaking
Unit 5	p. 6	Verbs as action words; past and present tenses
Unit 6	p. 7	Adjectives
Unit 7	p. 8	Words with *ck*
Unit 8	p. 9	A or an?
Unit 9	p. 10	Clues to meaning
Unit 10	p. 11	Synonyms

TERM 2

Unit 11	p. 12	Suffixes: *-ness, -ly, -ful*
Unit 12	p. 13	Verb agreement: *am, is, are, was, were*
Unit 13	p. 14	Punctuation
Unit 14	p. 15	More about adjectives
Unit 15	p. 16	Word building
Unit 16	p. 17	Word fun
Unit 17	p. 18	Silent letters
Unit 18	p. 19	Opposites
Unit 19	p. 20	Suffixes: *-er, -est*
Unit 20	p. 21	Key words

TERM 3

Unit 21	p. 22	Using a dictionary
Unit 22	p. 23	Prefixes and suffixes: *dis-, un-, non-, mis-, anti-; -ness, -ful, -y, -er, -est*
Unit 23	p. 24	Pronouns
Unit 24	p. 25	Using speech marks and other punctuation
Unit 25	p. 26	Homonyms
Unit 26	p. 27	Fiction and non-fiction
Unit 27	p. 28	Joining sentences
Unit 28	p. 29	Compound words
Unit 29	p. 30	Prefixes: *mis-, ex-*
Unit 30	p. 31	Proofreading
Revision	p. 32	Verb tense; pronouns; adjectives

THE COURSE COMPONENTS

Copymaster checklist

TERM 1

Unit 1	1	Collecting story openings
	2	Look, say, cover, write, check
	3	Words I know
Unit 3	4	Characters: cutouts for stick puppets
Unit 4	5	Collecting verbs
Unit 5	6	Presentation master: a home for a pet
Unit 6	7	Presentation master: poem on the senses
Unit 8	8	Presentation master: story based on *The Flat Man*
Unit 9	9	Collecting new words
Unit 10	10	Revision – term 1 assessment master

TERM 2

Unit 11	11	Story board (for planning writing or recording key incidents from reading)
	12	Fiction book review
Unit 12	13	Writing frame: a letter
Unit 13	14	Planning a story
	15	Book review: a story
Unit 15	16	Making notes
	17	Writing frame: a recipe
Unit 16	18	Boards for Achi and Nine Men's Morris
	19	Writing frame: rules for a board game
Unit 20	20	Revision – term 2 assessment master

TERM 3

Unit 23	21	Book review: plot, theme
	22	Book review: incident; language; behaviour of character
Unit 24	23	Finding out about an author: Roald Dahl
	24	Comparing books by the same author
Unit 26	25	Finding fiction books
	26	Finding non-fiction books
Unit 29	27	Collecting types and forms of humour
Unit 30	28	Collecting common expressions
	29	Self-assessment sheet
	30	Revision – term 3 assessment master

Teacher's Notes

Year 3 • Terms 1–3

TERM 1

HALF-TERMLY PLANNER

Year 3 • Term 1 • Weeks 1–5

SCHOOL _____ CLASS _____ TEACHER _____

		Phonetics, spelling and vocabulary	Grammar and punctuation	Comprehension and composition	Texts
Continuous work Weeks 1–5		WL 1, 2, 3, 4, 5, 6, 7, 13, 20, 21	SL 1, 10, 11, 12, 13	TL 9	**Range** **Fiction and poetry**: Stories with familiar settings; plays **Non-fiction**: Information text on topic of interest – non-chronological
Blocked work Week	Unit				Titles
1	1		SL 2, 6, 11, 12	TL 1, 2, 3, 11	From *The Moving Mystery*, Carmen Harris
2	2	WL 8, 9	SL 2, 7, 11	TL 1, 2, 3, 8, 11	From *Philomena Hall and the Best Kept Gerbil Competition*, Roy Apps; From *The Postbox Mystery*, Robert Swindells
3	3		SL 2, 6, 19	TL 2, 4, 5, 14	From *The School Bell*, Jacquie Buttriss and Ann Callander; From *No Entry – Two Short Plays for Seven to Eight Parts*, Jan Carew
4	4	WL 10, 11, 12, 19	SL 2, 3, 5, 7, 8	TL 1, 2, 3, 5, 8, 10	From *The Trouble with Mice*, Pat Moon
5	5		SL 3, 4, 5	TL 2, 8, 16, 17, 20, 22	From *Walking the Goldfish*, Michael Hardcastle; *Setting up an Aquarium*

HALF-TERMLY PLANNER

TERM 1

Year 3 • Term 1 • Weeks 6–10

SCHOOL _____ CLASS _____ TEACHER _____

		Phonetics, spelling and vocabulary	Grammar and punctuation	Comprehension and composition	Texts
Continuous work **Weeks 6–10**		WL 1, 2, 3, 4, 5, 6, 7, 13, 20, 21	SL 1, 10, 11, 12, 13	TL 9	**Range** **Fiction and poetry**: Stories with familiar settings; poems based on observation and the senses; shape poems **Non-fiction**: Information texts on topics of interest; non-chronological report; thesauruses, dictionaries
Blocked work **Week**	**Unit**				**Titles**
6	6	WL 16, 17, 18		TL 6, 7, 8, 9, 12	*Jigsaw Puddle*, Emily Hearn; *Ice Cream and Fizzy Lemonade*, Stanley Cook; *Smells*, A. Elliott-Cannon; *Sounds*, Alexander Kennedy; *The Feel of Things*, A. Elliott-Cannon; *What is Red?*, Mary O'Neill
7	7	WL 6		TL 9, 17, 18, 19, 20, 22	From *Diwali*, Kerena Marchant; From *High Days and Holidays*, David Self
8	8	WL 8, 10, 11, 12	SL 4	TL 1, 8, 11, 15, 17	From *The Flat Man*, Rose Impey; *I Can't Get to Sleep*, Richard Burns
9	9	WL 13, 14, 15		TL 9, 17, 19, 20, 21, 22	From *The Nature Trail Book of Birdwatching*, Usborne
10	10	WL 16		TL 6, 7, 8, 12, 13	*one*, e.e. cummings; *Snake*, Keith Bosley; *Sky Day Dream*, Robert Froman; *Mosquito*, Marie Zbierski; *O my!*, Anon; *Whoosh!*, Max Fatchen

Focus on Literacy Teacher's Resource Book 3 © Barry and Anita Scholes, HarperCollins*Publishers* Ltd 1999

Unit 1 — Charlie and Ben Move House

Key Learning Objectives

TL1	To identify the setting and select words and phrases that describe it
TL2	To investigate how dialogue is presented in stories, through statements, questions and exclamations; how paragraphing is used to organise dialogue
TL3	To be aware of the different voices used in stories using dramatised readings, showing the differences between the narrator and different characters used
TL11	To write a short description of a known place
SL2	To take account of grammar and punctuation when reading aloud
SL6	To secure knowledge of question marks, understand their purpose and use appropriately in own writing
SL11	To write in complete sentences
SL12	To demarcate the end of sentences with a full stop and the start of a new one with a capital letter

Range:	Story with familiar setting
Texts:	From *The Moving Mystery*, Carmen Harris
Resources:	Big Book 3A pp. 4–7
	Pupil's Book 3 pp. 2–4
	Homework Book 3 p. 2: Capital letters, full stops and question marks
	Copymaster 1: Collecting story openings
	Copymaster 2: Look, say, cover, write, check
	Copymaster 3: Words I know

DAY 1

Big Book pp. 4–5; Pupil's Book p. 3

Shared reading

- In the Big Book the first text of each unit is the main text which forms the focus of shared reading on days 1 and 2, and the stimulus for shared writing on day 3. The *To think and talk about* questions will help both you and the children to focus on key aspects of the text. Further teaching points are listed below.
- Encourage the children to follow the extract as you read it aloud. As you do so, make the children aware of the voices used in the story, showing the differences between the narrator and the different characters.
- Investigate the first sentence of the story: "Rat-tat-tat!". Does this make the children want to read on? Why?
- Copymaster 1 is for the children to collect interesting story openings.
- Talk about the description of Charlie's special friend. Look at their conversation. Make sure that the children appreciate the dialogue is really Charlie talking to himself, and that it shows Charlie's feelings about moving. Encourage the children to identify those feelings, and to justify their reponses with evidence from the text.

- Ask the children to look for clues about the setting. Which words and phrases tell us about Charlie's present home? Do any children live in a similar home? What does the text reveal about Charlie's new home? How will it be different?
- Show the children how to use words in the question to start off their answers.

Focused word/sentence work

- Look at the different dialogue functions: questions, exclamations and statements. Examine the use of capital letters, full stops and commas.
- Note the use of capitalisation for names and the first words of sentences. Ask why "Estate Agents" and "Sold" have capital letters.

Independent work

- To help with differentiation the work is usually divided into two, three or four sections, A, B, C or D, A being the easiest and D the hardest. It is important that these activities are carefully matched to the children's ability, and fully explained to them before they begin, so that you are able to work with your group without breaking off to provide further support.
- Children work on the comprehension questions on page 3 of the Pupil's Book. To help with differentiation the work is in two sections.

Plenary

- Review the children's independent text work. Explain how to use the text to find literal answers, and how to use clues where information is not given directly.

DAY 2

Big Book pp. 4–5; Pupil's Book, p. 3

Shared reading work

- Examine how speech is punctuated. Introduce the term "speech marks".
- Investigate how paragraphing is used to organise dialogue.
- Read the story as a play with one or more narrators and others to read the dialogue.
- Point out the clues to how some words are spoken: "said Ben grumpily".

Focused word/sentence work

- Focus on the dialogue. Introduce the term "speech marks". Look at how speech marks separate the actual words spoken, and how words such as *said*, *cried* and *asked* are used to introduce and conclude dialogue.
- Investigate the use of question marks in the text. What is their function? Where are they placed in a sentence? Point out where they are placed when speech marks are used.

Independent work

- Introduce the work in the Pupil's Book on writing sentences by revising the use of capital letters and full stops. Point out that besides being properly punctuated sentences must make complete sense.

Plenary

- Ask the children to read aloud some of the sentences they have written. Do they make complete sense?
- Review the presentation of dialogue in stories.

DAY 3
Pupil's Book p. 4

Shared writing

- Ask the children to study the picture on page 4 in the Pupil's Book. Then read together the description of the house. Encourage the children to suggest suitable words or phrases to complete the description.
- Is there any other detail which might have been included? Ask the class to compose suitable sentences.

Focused word/sentence work

- Ask the children to think about their own home, or a house they know well. Using the passage as a guide, ask them to suggest suitable words and phrases to describe its outside appearance. Make a list of their suggestions.
- Demonstrate how the description in the Pupil's Book may be used as a model for the children's own writing. Show them how to combine suitable words and phrases from the list with sentence models from the text. Explain how sentences may be changed to suit a different description. Encourage the composition of entirely new sentence constructions, as appropriate.

Independent work

- Ask the children to write their own descriptions following the writing process you have demonstrated. It is not essential that the children complete the work in this session. Ask the children to treat this as a first draft. A second or final draft may be written as independent work on day 4.

Plenary

- Review the descriptions written by the class. Encourage the children to suggest aspects which may be corrected or improved in a second draft.

DAY 4
Big Book pp. 6–7; Pupil's Book p. 4

Shared reading

- Read the second extract from the Charlie story. Ask the class in what ways the two neighbourhoods are different. Encourage them to use words and phrases from the text when answering.

Focused word/sentence work

- Point out the use of commas to separate items in the list of places seen by Ben and Charlie from the car.
- Review the first draft descriptions written on day 3. Select suitable examples which show good practice. Ask for suggestions for improving spelling, punctuation and grammar. Demonstrate the use of a dictionary for checking spellings.
- Show how the "look, say, cover, write, check" strategy may be used for learning new spellings.

- Copymaster 2 is a useful reference and practice sheet for this strategy.
- Copymaster 3 may be used as a spelling log for spellings mastered.

Independent work

- Ask the children to write a second draft of their descriptions.

Plenary

- Ask the children to read aloud their descriptions. Discuss what makes the best descriptions successful, e.g. well-chosen words, interesting sentences, etc.

DAY 5
Big Book pp. 6–7; Pupil's Book p. 4

Shared reading

- Read again the second text on pages 6–7 in the Big Book. Ask children to read it aloud, taking account of grammar and punctuation.
- Encourage the children to express their views about the story. Will Charlie and Ben like their new home?
- Have any of the class moved house? How did they feel before the move, during the removal and afterwards? How easy was it to make new friends?

Focused word/sentence work

- Look at the first text again on page 2 of the Pupil's Book. Pick out the questions. How are they set out?
- Talk about the words which introduce the questions. A list of common question words is given on page 4, but ask the children to look for other ways of beginning questions, such as *can*, *did*, *are*, *is*, etc.
- Ask the children to invent questions about either text for others to answer. Revise the punctuation of statements and questions.

Independent work

- Children practise punctuating and composing questions.

Plenary

- Review the week's work. Consolidate appropriate teaching points.

Consolidation and extension

- Select suitable questions for the class to answer from those composed by the children.
- Copymaster 1 is a sheet for collecting story openings. As a collection is built up, encourage the children to use these formal elements in their own writing.
- Copymaster 2 is a useful reference and practice sheet for the "look, say, cover, write, check" spelling strategy.
- Copymaster 3 may be used as a spelling log for spellings the children have mastered.

Homework

- Page 2 in the Homework Book consolidates work on capital letters, full stops and question marks.

Unit 2 — An Exciting Letter

Key Learning Objectives

TL1	To identify the setting and select words and phrases that describe it
TL2	To be aware of how dialogue is presented in stories
TL3	To be aware of the different voices used in stories using dramatised readings, showing the differences between the narrator and different characters used
TL8	To express their views about a story, identifying specific words and phrases to support their viewpoint
TL11	To write a short description of a known place
SL2	To take account of grammar and punctuation when reading aloud
SL7	To understand the basic conventions of speech punctuation
SL11	To write in complete sentences
WL8	To investigate how the spelling of verbs alters when -ing is added
WL9	To investigate and learn to use the spelling pattern le

Range:	Stories with familiar settings
Texts:	From *Philomena Hall and the Best Kept Gerbil Competition*, Roy Apps From *The Postbox Mystery*, Robert Swindells
Resources:	Big Book 3A pp. 8–11 Pupil's Book 3 pp. 5–7 Homework Book 3 p. 3: Speech marks

DAY 1

Big Book pp. 8–9; Pupil's Book p. 6

Shared reading

- Read the extract aloud. Discuss why Jo should be so excited, and why she rushed to Annabelle's flat. Ask the class to pick out the words and phrases which describe the *setting*. Notice that the description begins with a general impression: "huge and bright", and the view from the window. It then goes on to tell us who was there and what they were doing.

- Ask the children in what ways this is similar to or different from their own living room. Encourage them to describe their own rooms.

Focused word/sentence work

- Discuss words in the text which are new to the children. Teach them strategies to decipher them, e.g. predicting from context, using knowledge of phonemes, graphic knowledge, etc.

- Examine the use of exclamation marks at the end of the extract. Discuss how exclamation marks and the word "yelled" convey the excitement of the announcement. Compare this with the earlier "'We're in the lounge,' said Annabelle." where the full stop denotes a statement, and the word "said" gives little indication of how she spoke.

- Remind the children how to answer questions about the passage by using words in the question to start off their answers. Encourage them to make up their own questions for others to answer in sentences.

Independent work

- Children answer the questions about the story on page 6 in the Pupil's Book, using complete sentences.

Plenary

- Review the children's independent text work. Demonstrate how to use the text to find literal answers, and how to use clues where information is not given directly.

DAY 2

Big Book pp. 8–9; Pupil's Book p. 6

Shared reading

- Look at the use of italics in the text. Point out that they are used to separate the words of Jo's letter from the narrative text.

- Draw attention to how the dialogue is set out, e.g. the use of speech marks and new lines for each speaker.

- Ask the children to improvise what Jo will tell the gang and what their responses might be. Present this as a picture sequence with speech bubbles and its corresponding equivalent in direct speech. Point out that the speech marks perform the same function as the speech bubble.

Focused word/sentence work

- Ask the children to pick out the verbs in the passage. Which are verbs of speech, e.g. *said*, *yelled*. How many other such words can the children think of?

- Investigate the spelling pattern -le in words such as *circle* and *middle*. How many other words can the children think of which have this pattern?

Independent work

- Children explore the use of speech marks.

- Children to investigate words ending in -le by completing the passage using words from the word bank. Suggest that those who finish early should use some of the words in sentences of their own.

Plenary

- Ask the children to suggest further words which have the -le spelling pattern.

DAY 3

Big Book pp. 8–9; Pupil's Book p. 7

Shared writing and focused word/sentence work

- Re-read the first extract, drawing the children's attention to the description of Annabelle's flat. Then study together page 7 in the Pupil's Book, which offers help in planning and writing a description of the room depicted. Using the picture and sketch plan in the book, ask the children to suggest suitable descriptive words and phrases. Write these down as a writing plan, and then work with the children to expand the notes into a full description. Refer to the description of Annabelle's room as necessary.

Independent work

- Ask the children to use the same approach to plan a description of their own living room. Ask them to aim to complete their plan within the session. The actual writing may be completed on day 4, or outside the literacy hour.

Plenary

- Discuss the children's choice of words for their descriptions. Ask the class to suggest more suitable words if necessary. Draw attention to the children's use of particularly apt or expressive language.

DAY 4

Big Book pp. 10–11; Pupil's Book p. 7

Shared reading

- Read aloud the extract from *The Postbox Mystery* on pages 10–11 in the Big Book, showing the differences between the narrator and the three characters.
- Does the class think the police believe Laura? What makes them think so? Which words and phrases give clues?

Focused word/sentence work

- Draw attention to how the dialogue is set out, e.g. the use of speech marks and new lines for each speaker. Note that we are not always told who is speaking each line. How can we tell who is saying the words?
- Compare this passage with the extract on pages 8–9 in the Big Book. Explain that speech marks may be double or single. It is recommended that the children use double speech marks in their own writing to avoid confusion with apostrophes.

Independent work

- Children use their plans from day 3 to write descriptions of their own living rooms.

Plenary

- Let the children read their descriptions aloud. Develop an atmosphere of constructive criticism, and provide feedback and encouragement.

DAY 5

Big Book pp. 10–11; Pupil's Book p. 7

Shared reading

- Draw attention to how the dialogue is set out, e.g. the use of speech marks and new lines for each speaker. Note that we are not always told who is speaking each line. How can we tell who is saying the words?
- Examine the dialogue again. Ask the children to pick out the questions and statements. Who asks most of the questions? What question does Laura ask?
- Ask four children to read the passage aloud, taking the parts of the narrator and the three characters.

Focused word/sentence work

- Explore further the use of speech marks. Draw attention to the use of capital letters to start direct speech, even in the middle of a sentence: *The policewoman said, "How old are you, love?"*
- Explain how direct speech is usually separated from words such as "said Laura" by a comma. In sentences which begin with spoken words the comma is placed immediately before the closing speech marks. Otherwise the comma comes before the opening speech marks.
- When a sentence begins with a spoken question, the question mark replaces the comma. This rule also applies to an exclamation mark. See the end of the first text on page 9 in the Big Book for an example of this: *"Wow!" yelled Annabelle.*
- Investigate verbs ending in *-ing*, e.g. *looking, wandering*. Short verbs with a single vowel double the last letter before adding *-ing*, e.g. *sitting, knitting*. Verbs ending in *-e* drop it before adding a suffix, e.g. *inviting, taking, staring*.

Independent work

- Children investigate how the spelling of verbs alters when *-ing* is added. Question 2 in each section requires the children to use *-ing* verbs in sentences of their own.

Plenary

- Review the week's work. Consolidate appropriate teaching points. Correct any misconceptions.

Homework

- Page 3 in the Homework Book has consolidation practice in using speech marks.

Unit 3 — The School Bell

Key Learning Objectives

TL2	To investigate how dialogue is presented, through statements, questions and exclamations
TL4	To read, prepare and present playscripts
TL5	To recognise key differences between prose and playscript
TL14	To write simple playscripts based on own reading and oral work
SL2	To take account of grammar and punctuation when reading aloud
SL6	To secure knowledge of question marks and exclamation marks, understand their purpose and use appropriately in own writing
SL19	To discuss common vocabulary for introducing and concluding dialogue

Range:	Plays
Texts:	From *The School Bell*, Jacquie Buttriss and Ann Callander, Collins
	From *No Entry – Two Short Plays for Seven to Eight Parts* by Jan Carew
Resources:	Big Book 3A pp. 12–17
	Pupil's Book 3 pp. 8–10
	Homework Book 3 p. 4: Different kinds of sentences
	Copymaster 4: Characters: cutouts for stick puppets

DAY 1
Big Book pp. 12–15; Pupil's Book p. 9

Shared reading
- Read the play to the children, allowing them to appreciate how the voice may be used to bring characters to life. Point out how settings are indicated in a playscript. Ask the children to think and talk about answers to the questions.
- Compare the playscript with the dialogue from *The Postbox Mystery* on pages 10–11 in the Big Book. Look at how the dialogue is set out: with the names of the characters at the beginning of their lines, and a new line for each speaker. Talk about the function of the narrator in this play. How is this different from the narrator in stories?

Focused word/sentence work
- Discuss the purpose of the exclamation mark when Miss Cross says "That's enough from you, Grant!" What does this tell us about the way she feels about Grant?
- Discuss words for *said* which might be used if this script were a story text.
  Examples: "Get off that wall," *ordered* Miss Cross.
  "We weren't teasing them," *answered* Ali.
  "Well, be nice to them," *replied* Miss Cross.
  "That's enough from you, Grant!" she *warned*.
  "But …" *protested* Grant.

Independent work
- Children answer the questions about the play on page 9 in the Pupil's Book.

Plenary
- Re-emphasise the differences between prose and playscripts.

DAY 2
Big Book pp. 12–15; Pupil's Book p. 9

Shared reading
- Ask children to read the script aloud. Encourage them to speak clearly and with appropriate intonation.
- Talk about what might have happened to the bell and what the teachers will do next.

Focused word/sentence work
- Revise statements, questions and exclamations. Let the children find one example of each in the playscript. Ask the children to find examples of orders. Notice that the question "Go and get me the bell, will you?" does not begin with a question word because it is an order with the added question tag *will you?*.
- Challenge the children in turn to give you a statement, e.g. about the classroom. Then ask them to invent questions, exclamations and orders.
- Ask the children to listen to the different intonations when the four kinds of sentence are spoken.

Independent work
- Activities on page 9 in the Pupil's Book will help the children to secure understanding of the purpose of exclamation marks, and to use them properly in their own writing.
- A second activity gives further practice on different kinds of sentences.

Plenary
- Experiment with speaking the same sentence as a statement, an order, a question and an exclamation, e.g. *You're going to school*. Notice the differences in intonation. Ask the class which punctuation marks correspond to the different inflections.

DAY 3
Big Book pp. 12–15; Pupil's Book p. 10

Shared writing
- Re-read the first playscript.
- Discuss the questions in the "How does the story end?" section. Use the children's ideas to develop a story plan continuing the play. Show how this plan can be used to write new lines of dialogue for all six characters, including the narrator.

Focused word/sentence work

- Ask the children to invent dialogue which includes statements, questions, exclamations and orders.

Independent work

- The children write their own script about the missing school bell. This will be continued on day 4.

Plenary

- Ask the children to read aloud lines from their writing. Provide feedback and encouragement.

DAY 4

Big Book pp. 16–17; Pupil's Book p. 10

Shared reading

- Read the playscript on pages 16–17 in the Big Book. How are the Potter-Smiths different from the Bakers? Are the Potter-Smiths being reasonable? Why not? Can the children suggest reasons why breakfast was late that morning?
- Ask the children how this script is different from the previous play: there is no narrator and so we are given stage directions describing the scene and the action. Notice how these are set out.

Focused word/sentence work

- Discuss words for *said* which might be used if this script were a story text.

    Examples: "Good morning," *greeted* the Potter-Smiths.
    "I must say I don't think much of this guest house," *complained* Mrs P-S.
    "I suppose it all depends on what you're used to," *commented* Mrs P-S.
    "Sorry, breakfast is a bit late today," *apologised* Stella.

Independent work

- Children continue writing their playscripts.

Plenary

- Ask the children to read aloud lines from their writing, with appropriate expression. Provide feedback and encouragement.

DAY 5

Big Book pp. 16–17; Pupil's Book p. 10

Shared reading

- Ask the children to read aloud the play set in the guest house, showing the differences between the snooty Potter-Smiths and the easy-going Bakers. Encourage the children to experiment with different ways of doing this.
- Ask some of those children who have completed their own playscripts to read them aloud. Again, encourage them to experiment with different ways of doing this.

Focused word/sentence work

- Discuss different ways of presenting speech: as plays, direct speech in stories, speech bubbles and captions in cartoons.
- Experiment with presenting lines from the play as speech bubbles. Point out that text in speech bubbles is always as short as possible. Discuss ways of shortening lines while retaining the meaning.

    Examples: We usually go to the Ritz Hotel, you know – We usually go to the Ritz
    Yes, they work very hard to look after us – They work very hard

Independent work

- Children collect examples of statements and questions from the *Breakfast at Seaview* script and make up examples of their own.
- Some children may need to complete their playscripts during this session.
- Those children who have finished their work might get into groups of six to prepare a presentation of their plays.

Plenary

- Review the week's work. Consolidate appropriate teaching points.

Consolidation and extension

- Let the children act out their scripts or present them as a puppet play. You may prefer to continue this, or reserve it for presentation, outside the literacy hour. Copymaster 4 has pictures of all six characters for colouring, cutting out, making into stick puppets and using to present the play. Some children may prefer puppet plays to acting out the parts themselves. Of course, both ways may be used if more than one script is to be presented.

Homework

- Page 4 in the Homework Book consolidates the writing of statements, questions, exclamations and orders.

Unit 4: A Cage for a Mouse

Key Learning Objectives

TL1 To identify the setting and select words and phrases that describe it

TL2 To investigate how dialogue is presented in stories, through statements, questions and exclamations; how paragraphing is used to organise dialogue

TL3 To be aware of the different voices used in stories using dramatised readings, showing the differences between the narrator and different characters used

TL5 To recognise key differences between prose and playscript

TL8 To express their views about a story, identifying specific words and phrases to support their viewpoint

TL10 To use reading as a model, to write own passages of dialogue

SL2 To take account of grammar and punctuation when reading aloud

SL3 To understand the function of verbs in sentences through:
noticing that sentences cannot make sense without them
collecting and classifying examples of verbs from reading and knowledge

SL5 To use the term "verb" appropriately

SL7 To understand the basic conventions of speech punctuation

SL8 To use the term "speech marks"

WL10 To recognise and spell common prefixes and how these influence word meanings, *un-*, *dis-*

WL11 To use their knowledge of prefixes to generate new words from root words, especially antonyms, happy/unhappy, appear/disappear

WL12 To use the term "prefix"

WL19 To be aware of common vocabulary for introducing and concluding dialogue; collecting examples from reading

Range:	Story with a familiar setting
Texts:	From *The Trouble with Mice*, Pat Moon
Resources:	Big Book 3A pp. 18–23
	Pupil's Book 3 pp. 11–13
	Homework Book 3 p. 5: Verbs for ways of speaking
	Copymaster 5: Collecting verbs

DAY 1

Big Book pp. 18–21; Pupil's Book p. 12

Shared reading

- Read the extract aloud. Where is it set? How can the class tell? Ask the class to think of words to describe Chris and the way he behaves.
- Let the children read the passage aloud with a narrator and two children for the roles of Mum and Chris. Investigate how Chris pursues the argument, even after Mum's "And that's final." What does he promise Mum if he gets the mouse? What prompts him to say, "Great! Then I'll go on, and on, and on, and on ..."?

Focused word/sentence work

- What do the children think *vermin* means? What clues are there in the passage?
- Teach the children what a verb is, and how it functions in a sentence, using examples from the text.
- Can a sentence make sense without a verb? Ask the children to test this out with sentences from the text.
- Experiment with changing verbs in sentences from the text, both to change the meaning and to retain it, e.g. Mary *saw* the back gate crash against its latch; He *sauntered* in.

Independent work

- Children answer the questions about the story.

Plenary

- Review the children's independent text work. Demonstrate how to use the text to find literal answers, and how to use clues where information is not given directly.

DAY 2

Big Book pp. 18–21; Pupil's Book p. 12

Shared reading

- Collect examples of statements, questions, orders and exclamations from the extract.
- Notice how paragraphing is used to organise the dialogue.
- Examine the key differences between the dialogue here and that of the playscripts in the previous unit, e.g. the use of speech marks in prose and the occasional omission of the speaker's identity.
- Note that in both prose and playscripts a new line is begun whenever a different person begins to speak.

Focused word/sentence work

- The passage is unusual in that it is written in the present tense. Compare this with the extracts in Units 1 and 2. Ask the children to experiment with changing part of the text into the past tense.
- Investigate alternative words for *said*, or in this case *says*, as used in the passage, e.g. *asks*, *threatens*, *yells*. Why are these more effective than *says*? What more information do they give us?

Independent work

- Children reinforce their knowledge of verbs by working on the activities on page 12 in the Pupil's Book.
- A second activity offers further practice in using, collecting and classifying alternative verbs for "said". Copymaster 5 will be useful as follow up to this activity.

Plenary

- Consolidate the children's understanding of verbs.
- Ask the children to classify alternative verbs for *said*, e.g. *speaking loudly, softly, harshly*.

DAY 3
Big Book pp. 18–21; Pupil's Book p. 13

Shared writing, including focused word/sentence work

- Revise the key differences between dialogue in prose and playscripts. Discuss how to rewrite as a playscript the dialogue on pages 18–21 of the Big Book.
- Read again the text on pages 18–21 of the Big Book. Ask the children to relate anecdotes of similar conversations they have had with parents. How often do they get their own way?
- Plan a real or imaginary conversation between a child and a parent about being allowed a pet. Brainstorm ideas. Show how these can be set out as a playscript, with the setting and characters made clear.

Independent work

- Children write their own playscripts.

Plenary

- Provide feedback and encouragement to the children on their writing progress.

DAY 4
Big Book pp. 22–23; Pupil's Book p. 13

Shared reading

- Read the second extract from *The Trouble with Mice*, on pages 22–23 in the Big Book.
- How does Mary behave when she discovers the mouse is missing?
- Can the children suggest how the mouse might have got out?
- Why does she think the worst will happen on Friday?
- Ask the children to improvise the scene when Mary tells Chris about the mouse.

Focused word/sentence work

- Consolidate direct speech by transcribing the most exciting part of the improvised confrontation.

Independent work

- Children to continue their writing from day 3.

Plenary

- Ask the children to read aloud, or act out, the dialogue from their playscripts.

DAY 5
Big Book pp. 18–23; Pupil's Book p. 13

Shared reading/writing

- Read both the extracts from *The Trouble with Mice*. Which part do the children like best? Why?
- Ask the children to read their favourite parts aloud.

Focused word/sentence work

- How does the prefix *dis-* influence meaning? e.g. disbelief. Experiment with adding *dis-* to other words to make antonyms, e.g. *obey, like, agree*.
- Encourage the children to use the term *prefix*.
- Explore the use and meaning of the prefix *un-*, e.g. *unfasten, unhappy, unimportant*.

Independent work

- Children explore the prefixes *dis-* and *un-* in the Pupil's Book.

Plenary

- Review the week's work with particular emphasis on verbs and speech punctuation.

Consolidation and extension

- Ask the children to prepare and read aloud their written conversations.
- Ask the children to write as a playscript part, or all, of the dialogue in the main text.
- Copymaster 5 is a sheet for collecting and classifying alternative verbs.

Homework

- Page 5 of the Homework Book focuses on verbs used in dialogue, e.g. *shout, whisper, ask, reply*.

Unit 5: Walking the Goldfish

Key Learning Objectives

TL2	To investigate how dialogue is presented in stories, through statements, questions and exclamations; how paragraphing is used to organise dialogue
TL8	To express their views about a story, identifying specific words and phrases to support their viewpoint
TL16	To understand the distinction between fact and fiction; to use the terms "fact", "fiction" and "non-fiction" appropriately
TL17	To notice differences in the style and structure of fiction and non-fiction writing
TL20	To read information passages, and identify main points or gist of text
TL22	To write simple non-chronological writing from known information, using notes to organise and present ideas
SL3	To understand the function of verbs in sentences through: experimenting with changing simple verbs in sentences and discussing their impact on meaning
SL4	To use verb tenses with increasing accuracy in speaking and writing
SL5	To use the term "verb" appropriately

Range:	Story with a familiar setting Non-chronological information text
Texts:	From *Walking the Goldfish*, Michael Hardcastle *Setting up an Aquarium*
Resources:	Big Book 3A pp. 24–27 Pupil's Book 3 pp. 14–17 Homework Book 3 p. 6: Verbs as action words: past and present tenses Copymaster 6: Presentation master for non-chronological writing

Preparation
- Make available for day 5 a selection of fiction and non-fiction books for an investigation of their features.

DAY 1
Big Book pp. 24–25; Pupil's Book p. 15

Shared reading
- Read the extract on pages 24–25 in the Big Book. Why does Harry's dad say it is impossible for him to be bored? What does Harry think of this?
- Why do the children think Dad suggests taking the goldfish for a walk? Do they think he really expects Harry to do so?
- What do they think Harry will do next?

Focused word/sentence work
- Investigate the function of verbs in the passage. Ask the children to pick out the verbs in selected sentences.
- Explain the difference between the present and past tenses. Compare the use of the present tense in the non-chronological text with the fiction text. Note that the dialogue in *Walking the Goldfish* uses present tense verbs, while the narrative is past tense.
- Draw attention to how verbs change when forming the past tense:
  - by adding -*ed*, e.g. *answered, switched, wondered*
  - verbs ending in -*e* drop it before adding -*ed*, e.g. *glanced*
  - some verbs double the last letter before adding -*ed*, e.g. *spotted, grinned*
  - many verbs do not add -*ed*, but change their form instead, e.g. *stood, said, gave, began, was*.

Independent work
- Children answer questions about the story.

Plenary
- Review the children's independent text work. Demonstrate how to use the text to find literal answers, and how to use clues where information is not given directly.

DAY 2
Big Book pp. 24–25 and 26–27; Pupil's Book p. 15

Shared reading
- Read the non-fiction text on pages 26–27 of the Big Book. Explain how to use the emphasised *key words* in the *To think and talk about* questions and the headings in the text to help them find and discuss the main points.
- Explain the terms *fact*, *fiction* and *non-fiction*. Compare the aquarium text with *Walking the Goldfish* on pages 24–25. Which of the two texts is fact and which fiction? How can they tell?
- Discuss the differences in the style and structure of the fiction and non-fiction texts, looking at such things as dialogue and the use of the past tense in the fiction extract, and headings and the present tense in the non-fiction example.

Focused word/sentence work
- Experiment with alternative verbs which retain meaning, e.g. He *looked* round the room and *noticed* the goldfish bowl.
- Invent sentences with verbs which can be changed to an opposite meaning, e.g. Flat-topped cars *whizzed/crawled* past each other; He *picked up/put down* the goldfish bowl; His dad *grinned/scowled*.

Independent work
- Verbs are explored further on page 15 in the Pupil's Book: changing to an opposite meaning and retaining meaning.

- The verb cloze passage is a further short extract from the story. Any verb which fits the context is acceptable, but the actual words used by the author are given here for reference: 1) lived 2) lift 3) remembered 4) put 5) changed 6) wasn't 7) carry 8) had 9) grinned 10) did.

Plenary
- Review the children's cloze work.

DAY 3
Big Book pp. 26–27; Pupil's Book pp. 16–17

Shared writing/focused word work
- Explain that you are going to use the aquarium text (on pages 26–27 in the Big Book and page 17 in the Pupil's Book) as a model for writing about a home for a different kind of pet. Draw particular attention to the layout and the use of the present tense.
- Read each paragraph and ask the children how it might be changed to tell about setting up a cage for a gerbil, guinea pig or mouse. Use the headings in the planner in the Pupil's Book for making notes.

Independent work
- The children make their own notes for writing a non-chronological report on a home for a pet of their choice.

Plenary
- Provide feedback and encouragement to the children on their writing progress.

DAY 4
Big Book pp. 26–27; Pupil's Book pp. 16–17

Shared reading
- Experiment with changing the non-fiction text to a story with Harry and his dad having to set up an aquarium.
- Discuss with the children what might happen when Harry takes his goldfish for a walk, concentrating on what people might say.
- Improvise dialogue.

Focused word/sentence work
- Pick out examples of statements, questions and exclamations from the text.
- Revise the use of question and exclamation marks.
- Why are some words in the dialogue printed in italics? What effect does this have?

Independent work
- Children continue work on their "home for a pet" report.
- This activity may be extended by asking children to draw a labelled diagram of the cage.
- Copymaster 6 is a presentation sheet for the children's final draft.
- Those who have finished this writing may continue the story of Harry's walking the goldfish, in the form of a picture story with dialogue captions, as outlined on page 16 in the Pupil's Book.

Plenary
- Ask the children to read out their completed writing, or review work in progress, offering help and encouragement.

DAY 5
Big Book pp. 24–25; Pupil's Book p. 17

Shared reading
- Read both texts again to reinforce the children's understanding of the distinction between fiction and non-fiction.
- Show the children the examples of fiction and non-fiction texts you have collected (see **Preparation** opposite). Compare the two kinds, with particular emphasis on features such as contents, index, headings, sub-headings, illustrations, bibliographies, front and back covers, jacket blurb and information on authors.
- What clues to a book's content do we get from covers?

Focused word/sentence work
- Revise how the spelling of verbs changes when forming the past tense.
- Can the children suggest verbs which do not change, e.g. *cut, set*?

Independent work
- Page 17 in the Pupil's Book has work on verb tense.

Plenary
- Review and consolidate the main teaching points of the week's work.

Consolidation and extension
- Examine a selection of fiction and non-fiction texts, commenting on differences in style and structure (see **Preparation** opposite).
- Copymaster 6 is a presentation sheet for the children's final draft of their "home for a pet" work.

Homework
- Page 6 in the Homework Book gives further practice in recognising the use of verbs in sentences, and in changing verbs into the simple past tense.

Unit 6 — The Senses

Key Learning Objectives

TL6 To read aloud and recite poems, discussing choice of words and phrases that describe and create impact, with special emphasis on adjectives

TL7 To distinguish between rhyming and non-rhyming poetry and comment on the impact of the layout

TL8 To express their views about a poem, identifying specific words and phrases to support their viewpoint

TL9 To generate ideas relevant to a topic by brainstorming, word association, etc.

TL12 To collect suitable words and phrases, in order to write poems and short descriptions

WL16 To understand the purpose and organisation of a thesaurus, and to make use of it to find synonyms

WL17 To generate synonyms for high-frequency words

WL18 To use the term "synonym"

Range:	Poems based on observation and the senses
Texts:	*Jigsaw Puddle*, Emily Hearn; *Ice Cream and Fizzy Lemonade*, Stanley Cook; *Smells* and *The Feel of Things*, Rev. A. Elliott-Cannon; *Sounds*, Alexander Kennedy; *What is Red?*, Mary O'Neill
Resources:	Big Book 3A pp. 28–31 Pupil's Book 3 pp. 18–21 Homework Book 3 p. 7: Adjectives Copymaster 7: Presentation master for a poem on the senses

Preparation

- Collect further poems on observation and the senses to supplement those in the Big Book.
- Make available for days 2 and 3 a suitable thesaurus, such as *Collins Junior Thesaurus*.

DAY 1

Big Book pp. 28–29; Pupil's Book p. 19

Shared reading

- Read the poems on pages 28–29 in the Big Book.
- Discuss the content of each poem. Which senses are used to focus on the subject matter?
- What feelings do the poems give?
- Encourage the children to comment on the layout of the poems. How are they arranged on the page? Why do they end where they do? Do they have a regular rhythm? Do they rhyme? Investigate the rhyming scheme, e.g. *Jigsaw Puddle* – ABAACAD.

Focused word/sentence work

- Look at the use of adjectives in *Ice Cream and Fizzy Lemonade*. Ask the children to brainstorm other words to describe them, e.g. *white, clear, bubbly, sweet, creamy, tingly, refreshing*.
- Explore the use of powerful and expressive verbs, e.g. *sloshing, jiggle, bobble, prickles, tickles, tingles*. Discuss why they are particularly expressive.

Independent work

- Children answer questions on the poems (page 19 in the Pupil's Book).

Plenary

- Review the children's independent text work, showing them how to find answers from the text.

DAY 2

Big Book pp. 28–29; Pupil's Book p. 19

Shared reading

- Ask the children to read the poems aloud.
- Discuss the choice of words and phrases. Ask the children to explain why the poet says jigsaw *puddle* instead of *puzzle*. In what way is the puddle in the poem like a jigsaw puzzle? How does it get that way? What does "I fold the clouds in a sheep-like huddle" mean? How are the clouds like sheep? What is the puddle compared to at the end of the poem? Do the children think this is a good comparison? Why?
- Compare the effect of eating ice cream with that of drinking lemonade. Which words does the poet use? Compare the words *prickles, tickles* and *tingles* with *soft, smooth* and *soothing*. Why has the poet chosen such opposite words?

Focused word/sentence work

- Introduce the children to the term "synonym". Explain that *prickles, tickles* and *tingle* are all synonyms. They have *almost* the same meaning. Brainstorm other similar words, e.g. *itching, stinging, pins and needles*.
- Show them how synonyms can be found in a thesaurus. Explain that the purpose of a thesaurus is to help writers find a more interesting or precise word.

Independent work

- The children will need a thesaurus for the work on synonyms on page 19 in the Pupil's Book.

Plenary

- Consolidate synonyms by brainstorming synonyms for high-frequency words, e.g. *big, little, like, good, nice*. Ask the children to use a thesaurus when they run out of ideas.

DAY 3

Big Book pp. 29–31; Pupil's Book p. 20

Shared reading/writing (incorporating focused word work)

- Read the poems *Smells, Sounds, The Feel of Things* and *What is Red?* Explain that these are list poems, and investigate how they are constructed.
- Choose one of the poems as a model for shared writing.
- Brainstorm suitable ideas and write them down.
- Ask the children which ideas and words are most effective and why.
- Encourage the use of a thesaurus for more interesting or precise words.
- Select the best ideas. Place importance on quality over quantity.
- Discuss ways of arranging the ideas to best effect as a list poem.

Independent work

- Ask the children to write their own list poem, or complete the group poem. Remind them to refer both to the original poem as model and to the list poem planner on page 20 in the Pupil's Book.

Plenary

- Evaluate the group poem with the children. How well does it read aloud? How might it be improved?

DAY 4

Big Book p. 29–31; Pupil's Book p. 20

Shared reading

- Ask the children to read aloud the poems on pages 29–31 in the Big Book.
- Which lines do they think are particularly effective? Why?

Focused word/sentence work

- Collect and classify the sounds in the poem *Sounds* into loud and soft; man-made sounds, the sounds of birds, animals and insects, and weather sounds.
- Ask the children to suggest more pleasant sounds for each list.
- Investigate the spelling pattern *-le*, e.g. *puddle, bobble, huddle, muddle, bubbles*.

Independent work

- Children continue work on their list poems.
- Copymaster 7 is a presentation sheet for the pupils' poems.

Plenary

- Provide feedback and encouragement to the children on their writing progress.

DAY 5

Big Book pp. 28–31; Pupil's Book p. 21

Shared reading

- Ask the children to select their favourite poems from this unit and to read them aloud.
- Discuss reasons for their choices.
- Which are their favourite lines from the poems? Why?
- Which poem did they like least? Why?
- Read the poems you have collected on a similar theme (see **Preparation** opposite). Compare different views of the same subject.
- Encourage the children to make a big book of poems on observation and the senses, to include the best of the children's own poems.

Focused word/sentence work

- Look at the use of adjectives in the poems in this unit. Classify them according to the five senses.
- Ask the children to suggest words with similar meaning to those used in the poem, e.g. *fizzy/bubbly; smooth/creamy; muddle/jumble; sliding/slipping*.
- Prepare for the independent work on adjectives in the Pupil's Book (B, C and D) by explaining how to use commas in a list of words.

Independent work

- Children consolidate work on adjectives on page 21 in the Pupil's Book.

Plenary

- Read, enjoy and evaluate the children's own poems. Praise good use of adjectives and strong verbs.

Consolidation and extension

- Consolidate the work on adjectives by asking the children to brainstorm words for common objects. Encourage the children to consider all five senses.
- Copymaster 7 is a presentation sheet for the pupils' poems.

Homework

- Page 7 in the Homework Book focuses on adjectives.

Unit 7 Diwali

Key Learning Objectives

TL9 To generate ideas relevant to a topic by brainstorming, word association, etc.
TL17 To notice differences in the style and structure of fiction and non-fiction writing
TL18 To locate information using contents
TL19 To compare the way information is presented
TL20 To read information passages, and identify main points or gist of text
TL22 To write simple non-chronological writing from known information, using notes to organise and present ideas
WL6 To spell by analogy with other known words, light, night, etc.

Range:	Information texts on topic of interest
Texts:	From *Diwali*, Kerena Marchant
	Contents page from *High Days and Holidays*, David Self
Resources:	Big Book 3A pp. 32–35
	Pupil's Book 3 pp. 22–24
	Homework Book 3 p. 8: Words with *ck*

Preparation

- Select non-fiction books on a variety of subjects for comparison, with particular focus on contents pages. These will be needed on day 5. One or two examples of fiction books with chapter listings will also be useful.

DAY 1
Big Book pp. 32–34; Pupil's Book p. 23

Shared reading

- Look at how the information on Diwali is presented. There are no sub-headings, but different aspects of the topic are described in different paragraphs. There is also a captioned diagram with further information on diwas.
- Ask the children to identify the main idea of each paragraph. This will help them in locating information. Then ask the children to use the key words underlined in *To think and talk about* to find answers to the questions.

Focused word/sentence work

- Look at the use of commas to separate items in a list: "the nights are cold, long and dark"; "the triumph of good over evil, light over darkness, life over death".
- Point out the spelling pattern *-le* in *temple*.

Independent work

- Children complete the cloze passage about Diwali, and answer the questions in B in complete sentences.

Plenary

- Review the cloze work.
- Consolidate teaching points.

DAY 2
Big Book pp. 32–34; Pupil's Book p. 23

Shared reading

- Compare the way the information is presented with that of the non-fiction text in Unit 5. How is it similar or different? Which information is easier to use? Why?
- Explain how to identify the main points of a text by focusing on paragraph 2 and picking out the key words. Ask the children to do the same with paragraph 3.
- The main idea of paragraph 3 is that the dark nights are lit up. Ask the children to list the four ways this is done.

Focused word/sentence work

- Investigate how the spelling of verbs alters when *-ing* is added, e.g. *setting, celebrating, preparing, welcoming*. The same rules apply when adding *-ed*.
- Show how words can be spelled by analogy, e.g. *night, bright, light; dark, mark, park*.
- Discuss alternative words for *nice* and *get* as preparation for the independent work in the Pupil's Book.

Independent work

- Children experiment with generating synonyms for the high-frequency words *got* and *nice* on page 23 in the Pupil's Book.
- Children practise spelling *-ight* words by analogy.

Plenary

- Discuss the children's choice of synonyms for *nice* and *get*.

DAY 3
Pupil's Book p. 24

Shared writing/focused word/sentence work

- Look together at the different festivals listed on page 24 in the Pupil's Book. Discuss ones the children know well.
- Choose one of these and use the planner as a structure for discussing it in detail. The planner helps to organise ideas into three paragraphs. Concentrate on each paragraph in turn and make notes under the headings given. Show how the notes for the first paragraph can be used to write an introduction.

Independent work

- Ask the children to continue the writing you have begun, using the notes you have written.
- Alternatively, ask the children to choose a different festival and to plan their writing by making their own notes.

Plenary

- Review the work in progress, offering advice and encouragement. Draw attention to good practice.

DAY 4

Big Book p. 35; Pupil's Book p. 24

Shared reading

- Talk about the function of a contents page. How useful is it? What does it tell us about a book? Does it tell us all we need to know to find the information we might need?
- Explore the contents page on page 35 in the Big Book. What kind of book is it from? Practise answering questions about chapters and page numbers.

Focused word/sentence work

- Look at the use of capital letters in proper nouns, e.g. *St Nicholas*, *Ash Wednesday*, *Christmas Day*.
- Show how to distinguish between common and proper nouns. Ask the class to suggest a variety of proper nouns, e.g. the names of places, people, days of the week and months of the year, special days, brand names.
- Look at capitalisation in book, chapter, film and song titles.

Independent work

- Children continue or complete their writing.

Plenary

- Review the purposes of a contents page.

DAY 5

Big Book p. 35; Pupil's Book p. 24

Shared reading

- Compare the contents page on page 35 in the Big Book with that on page 24 in the Pupil's Book, and those of the books you have selected (see **Preparation** opposite).
- Compare non-fiction contents pages with the chapter list pages of fiction books. Point out that their function is similar.
- Examine other parts of non-fiction books, e.g. index, headings, sub-headings, page numbers, diagrams, bibliograpies. Discuss their functions.

Focused word/sentence work

- Investigate captions, headings and inset text in the non-fiction books. Explore their purposes. Ask the children to collect examples from a range of books.

Independent work

- Page 24 in the Pupil's Book gives practice in using the contents page of a non-fiction book.

Plenary

- Ask the children to read or talk about their work on festivals. This will be especially interesting if you have children from a variety of cultures.

Homework

- Page 8 in the Homework Book encourages spelling by analogy with known words ending in *-ck*.

Unit 8 The Flat Man

Key Learning Objectives

TL1	To identify the setting and select words and phrases that describe it
TL8	To express their views about a story, identifying specific words and phrases to support their viewpoint
TL11	To develop the use of settings in own stories by writing in the style of a familiar story, and using a sentence for a story opening
TL15	To begin to organise stories into paragraphs
TL17	To notice differences in the style and structure of fiction and non-fiction writing
SL4	To use verb tenses with increasing accuracy. Use past tense for narration.
WL8	To investigate how the spellings of verbs alter when -ing is added
WL10	To recognise and spell common prefixes and how these influence word meanings, de-, re-, pre-
WL11	To use their knowledge of prefixes to generate new words from root words
WL12	To use the term "prefix"

Range:	Story with a familiar setting; poem
Texts:	From *The Flat Man*, Rose Impey, Collins *I Can't Get to Sleep*, Richard Burns
Resources:	Big Book 3A pp. 36–39 Pupil's Book 3 pp. 25–27 Homework Book 3 p. 9: A or an? Copymaster 8: Presentation master: story based on *The Flat Man*

DAY 1
Big Book pp. 36–37; Pupil's Book p. 26

Shared reading

- Look at the opening sentence of the story of *The Flat Man*. Notice how it sets the scene very economically. The same sentence also introduces us to the storyteller, the main character, and creates suspense with the words "I hear noises".

- The extract is another example of a story written in the present tense. In this particular case it is a useful device to enhance the suspense. The danger is made more real because it is happening as we read, not at some time in the past. When we read a first person account in the past tense, we know the storyteller survived any dangerous situation, but in a present tense account the worst things imaginable may still happen.

- The device works even though we know that *The Flat Man* is a deliberate invention of the storyteller. Why does he do this? Is it a sensible thing to do? Might the boy regret his invention? Encourage the children to give reasons for their answers.

Focused word/sentence work

- Look at the spoken words in the text. Remind the class of the use of speech marks and associated punctuation, and that in books speech marks may be double or single.

Independent work

- Children answer questions about the story.

Plenary

- Review the children's independent text work, showing them how to find answers from the text.

DAY 2
Big Book pp. 36–37; Pupil's Book p. 26

Shared reading

- Discuss the words and phrases that describe and create impact: "long, bony finger"; "he clings like a stretched out skin"; "he creeps in corners and drifts in the dark"; "shrivel up like a piece of paper"; "slips and slides in the shadows"; "dart over and slide into bed"; "breathing his icy breath".

- Explore the powerful and expressive verbs: *squeeze, cling, shrivel, slip, slide, dart, drifts*.

- Ask six or seven of the children to read the story aloud. One person might read only the words of the Flat Man. Experiment with different ways of doing this. Which works best? Why?

Focused word/sentence work

- Let the children experiment with transforming selected sentences from the passage into the past tense. Look at the words which are changed. Point out that these are verbs. Discuss how they are changed, e.g. adding *-ed* (*pull – pulled*), sometimes dropping the final *s* before doing so (*whispers – whispered*), or the irregular verbs which change in many different ways (*keep – kept, mean – meant, cling – clung, know – knew, hold – held*).

Independent work

- Children change extracts from *The Flat Man* from the present tense into the past tense on page 26 in the Pupil's Book.

Plenary

- Review the children's work on the past tense. Revise the main spelling rules.

DAY 3
Big Book pp. 36–37; Pupil's Book p. 27

Shared writing, focused word/sentence work

- How close is *The Flat Man* story to real life? Let the children relate anecdotes about lying in the dark, and hearing sounds which suggest frightening things. Have any of them felt like the boy in the story? Have any of them deliberately tried to turn noises they recognise into something more sinister?

- Work together with the children on a plan for a story based on *The Flat Man*. First make a list of everyday noises the children might hear while lying in bed. Then ask them what the noises make them think of. Encourage them to suggest expressive words and phrases. Make a list. Ask them how each of these frightening sounds makes them feel.
- Pick out the best of these ideas and write a plan for the story in four paragraphs. Each of the first three paragraphs will describe a sound, a frightening explanation for it and the feelings of the writer. The final paragraph will tell the outcome of the story.
- Discuss the use of tense. The present tense is more exciting for this kind of story. Why?

Independent work
- Children write their own stories.

Plenary
- Review and encourage the children's continuing writing.

DAY 4
Big Book pp. 38–39; Pupil's Book p. 27

Shared reading
- Read the poem *I Can't Get to Sleep* on page 38 in the Big Book. How is this poem similar to, and different from, *The Flat Man*? Who is making up explanations for the noises in the poem? Why is he doing this? Compare the purpose of the explanations: the boy is enjoying making up frightening explanations, while the father is making up equally exciting stories, but this time to calm the child's fears.
- Explore the use of expressive language: "fairies ... made of light and shadow with bodies that shine like angels"; "[the dragon's] scales drink in sunlight"; "[bows and arrows and swords] that glint on the air like dust ... studded with a thousand sparkling jewels". The imagery is of light, magic and beauty.

Focused word/sentence work
- Explore synonyms for *shine* and *sparkle*. *The Collins School Thesaurus* is a useful reference for this.

Independent work
- Children continue, or complete, their writing.
- Copymaster 8 is a presentation sheet for the pupil's final draft.

Plenary
- Review work in progress, and read aloud some of the best completed work.

DAY 5
Big Book p. 38; Pupil's Book p. 27

Shared reading
- Look at the pattern of the poem. Why do the lines end where they do? Does the poem rhyme? Does it have a strong rhythm?
- Ask the children to read the poem aloud.
- Look back at the everyday sounds you listed on day 3. Ask the children to suggest new explanations of a magical but comforting nature, as in the poem.

Focused word/sentence work
- Ask the children to pick out their favourite words and phrases from the poem. Encourage them to use some of these in sentences of their own.
- Talk about the meanings and uses of the prefixes *pre-*, *de-* and *re-*.

Independent work
- Children use their knowledge of the prefixes *pre-*, *de-* and *re-* to generate new words from root words on page 27 in the Pupil's Book.

Plenary
- Encourage the children to read their stories aloud.

Consolidation and extension
- Copymaster 8 is a presentation sheet for the pupils' final draft of their stories.

Homework
- Page 9 in the Homework Book explores the use of *a* and *an*. First make sure the children know what vowels and consonants are.

Unit 9 — Nesting Birds

Key Learning Objectives

TL9	To generate ideas relevant to a topic by brainstorming, word association, etc.
TL17	To notice differences in the style and structure of fiction and non-fiction writing
TL19	To compare the way information is presented
TL20	To read information passages, and identify main points or gist of text
TL21	To make a simple record of information from texts read
TL22	To write simple non-chronological writing from known information, using notes to organise and present ideas
WL13	To collect new words from reading and create ways of categorising and logging them
WL14	To infer meaning of unknown words from context
WL15	To have a secure understanding of the purpose and organisation of the dictionary

Range:	Information book on a topic of interest
Texts:	From *The Nature Trail Book of Birdwatching*, Usborne
Resources:	Big Book 3A pp. 40–43 Pupil's Book 3 pp. 28–31 Homework Book 3 p. 10: Clues to meaning Copymaster 9: Collecting new words

Preparation

- Make available a set of dictionaries, preferably *Collins Junior Dictionary* or *Collins School Dictionary*.
- The writing activities in this unit are planned to take place on days 2, 3 and 5.

DAY 1
Big Book pp. 40–41; Pupil's Book p. 29

Shared reading

- Examine how the information on nesting birds is presented: as text, diagrams and pictures. Compare this with the information texts in Units 5 and 7. How are they different? How useful are diagrams in giving information? In what other ways might the information on where birds nest be presented (e.g. as lists or a chart)?
- Encourage children to use the emphasised key words in the questions in *To think and talk about* to locate the answers to the questions.

Focused word/sentence work

- Explain to the children how the meaning of unfamiliar words can be inferred from context, e.g. *territory*.
- Ask the children to suggest definitions for words such as *bird, nest, beak, egg, season*, etc. Discuss their definitions. Has anything important been left out? Can the definition be made more precise, or concise?
- Ask the children to find these words in a dictionary, and compare their definitions with those given. How might the children's definitions be improved?

Independent work

- Page 29 in the Pupil's Book has questions on the text for the children to answer.

Plenary

- Review the children's independent text work, showing them how to find answers from the text.

DAY 2
Big Book pp. 40–41; Pupil's Book p. 29

Shared reading/writing

- The writing activities in this unit are planned to take place on days 2, 3 and 5.
- The first activity on page 29 in the Pupil's Book is for day 2, and the second for day 3.
- Explain to the class how information may be recorded as a chart. Show them how to do this by picking out the information about where birds nest from the diagram in the Big Book, and entering this in the chart format as shown in the Pupil's Book.

Focused word/sentence work

- Ask the children to find in the text examples of words with double consonants, e.g. *difficult, all, usually, collect, mallard, swallow, shallow, collared, territory, arrives, carrion crow, carrying, common, droppings, approaches*.

Independent work

- Children copy and complete the chart.

Plenary

- Encourage the children to test the usefulness of their charts by asking each other questions about where birds nest.

DAY 3
Big Book pp. 40–41; Pupil's Book pp. 29–30

Shared reading/writing

- Teach the children how to pick out key words in the text, and how these can be used to write simple notes. Look together at the later independent work on page 30 in the Pupil's Book, so that the children understand what they will have to do.
- Investigate the function and layout of the diagrams. Discuss the diagram work on page 30 in the Pupil's Book and show the class how to combine information from the two parts of the diagram on where birds nest.

Focused word/sentence work

- Note the use of commas in a list: They use thick bushes, trees, ivy-covered walls and sheds as nesting boxes.
- Examine other uses of commas in the text.

Independent work

- Children use the information on birds to make their own diagrams.

Plenary

- Review the children's diagrams.

DAY 4
Big Book pp. 42–43; Pupil's Book p. 30

Shared reading/writing

- Read the information text on bird spotting on pages 42–43 of the Big Book. Ask the children to comment on aspects of layout, i.e. illustrations and captions.
- Look for answers to the questions. Ask the children to first pick out the key words in the questions, and to scan for these in the text.

Focused word/sentence work

- Discuss the purpose and organisation of a dictionary. Challenge the children to quickly find words connected with birds, e.g. *owl, eagle, claw, wing*.

Independent work

- Children investigate clues to meaning on page 30 in the Pupil's Book.
- The second activity focuses on finding the main points of a text by picking out the key words.

Plenary

- Review the work on inferring meaning from context. The full definitions may be checked in a dictionary such as *Collins School Dictionary*.
- Ask the children to review their notes. Do the notes include all the main points?

DAY 5
Big Book pp. 40–43; Pupil's Book p. 31

Shared reading/writing, including word/sentence work

- Compare the different ways of presenting information shown in this unit.
- Ask the children to use their own charts to answer questions, e.g. Where does a wren nest? Which birds nest in sheds and houses?
- Ask similar questions using the diagram in the Big Book, e.g. Where does a nuthatch nest? Which birds nest in hedges?
- Ask the children to use either the diagram or the chart to answer these questions: Which birds nest in gardens? Which garden birds nest in trees? Do dunnocks and long-tailed tits nest in similar places? Which tree-nesting birds do not usually nest in gardens?
- Which text did they use to find the answers? Why was this?
- What information does the diagram tell us that the chart does not?
- Discuss why one way of presenting information is sometimes better than another.

- Show the children how to draw together information from the diagram in the main text and the bird spotting information on pages 42–43 of the Big Book to complete the chart on page 31 in the Pupil's Book.

Independent work

- Children use information in both texts to complete a chart on bird spotting.

Plenary

- Ask the children to ask each other questions to which their charts on bird spotting provide the answers.
- Review the week's work.

Consolidation and extension

- Give further practice in making notes by asking the children to write simple notes on the passage in Unit 5: *Setting up an aquarium*.
- Copymaster 9 encourages the children to collect new words from their reading. This will help them in spelling the word and finding the meaning in a dictionary.

Homework

- Page 10 in the Homework Book gives further practice in using context clues to deduce the meaning of a new word. Encourage the children to use a dictionary to check each meaning after they have finished the work.

Unit 10 Shape Poems

Key Learning Objectives

TL6 To read aloud and recite poems, discussing choice of words and phrases that describe and create impact

TL7 To distinguish between rhyming and non-rhyming poetry and comment on the impact of the layout

TL8 To express their views about a poem, identifying specific words and phrases to support their viewpoint

TL12 To collect suitable words and phrases, in order to write poems and short descriptions

TL13 To invent calligrams and a range of shape poems, selecting appropriate words and careful presentation

WL16 To understand the purpose and organisation of a thesaurus, and to make use of it to find synonyms

Range:	Shape poems
Texts:	*Sky Day Dream*, Robert Froman; *one*, e.e. cummings; *Snake*, Keith Bosley; *Mosquito*, Marie Zbierski; *Whoosh!*, Max Fatchen; *O my!*, Anon
Resources:	Big Book 3A pp. 44–48 Pupil's Book 3 pp. 32–34 Homework Book 3 p. 11: Synonyms Copymaster 10: Revision – assessment master for term 1

Preparation

- Make available a thesaurus, preferably *Collins Junior Thesaurus*, for day 2.
- There is a writing activity for each day in this unit.

DAY 1

Big Book pp. 44–47; Pupil's Book p. 33

Shared reading

- Read and discuss the shape poems on pages 44–47 in the Big Book.
- How is each poem arranged on the page? How does the shape match the words?
- What does each poem describe? Pick out words and phrases which you think are particularly effective.

Focused word/sentence work

- Pick out the verbs in the poems. Which poems have verbs in the present tense? Which in the past? Which has no verbs at all? How does the poem make sense without a verb? Although there is no verb in *Mosquito*, there is action. What is this action? How does the poet show this?
- e.e. cummings chose to write his poems, even his name, without capital letters. Where in the poem would capital letters normally be used?

Independent work

- Introduce the children to the term *calligram*: a word, sentence or poem in which the calligraphy, formation of letters or font represents an aspect of the poem's subject.
- There are examples of calligrams on page 33 in the Pupil's Book to encourage the children to make their own single word calligrams.

Plenary

- Discuss the calligrams the children have written. Which work best? Why?

DAY 2

Big Book pp. 44–47; Pupil's Book p. 33

Shared reading

- Read the poems on pages 44–47 of the Big Book again. Which poem is based on a single word calligram? How does the poet achieve the pattern with just a single word?
- Which poem do the children like best? Least? Encourage them to give reasons for their answers.
- Ask the children to read the poems aloud. Do the poems work as well when read aloud? How much do the shapes of the poems contribute to their appeal?

Focused word/sentence work

- Look at the verbs of movement used in the poems, e.g. *glides, fly, alight*. Use a thesaurus to explore synonyms for *fly*. Which of these might replace *fly off* in the *Sky Day Dream* poem?
- Experiment with using the other synonyms for *fly* in the children's own sentences.

Independent work

- The activities on page 33 in the Pupil's Book focus on calligrams and calligram sentences. Please make a thesaurus and dictionary available for this work.

Plenary

- Review the children's work.

DAY 3

Big Book pp. 44–47; Pupil's Book p. 34

Shared reading/writing and focused word/sentence work

- Look at the poems on pages 44–47 of the Big Book again. Which one is a calligram sentence? How is it similar to or different from the children's own calligram sentences?
- What is it that makes a calligram sentence into a poem? Is it just the shape, the words used or a combination of both? Discuss aspects such as the choice of words and phrases that describe and create impact. Why for example did e.e. cummings use the word "alights" instead of "falls"? Why is it a more suitable word?

- Look at the ideas and suggestions for the children's own shape poems. Choose a subject to work on as shared writing. Demonstrate the writing process from planning to final draft.

Independent work

- Ask the children to choose a subject for their own shape poem.

Plenary

- Let the children present their draft or finished poems to the class for discussion and appreciation.

DAY 4

Big Book p. 48; Pupil's Book p. 34

Shared reading

- Read the poem *Whoosh!* on page 48 in the Big Book. Why does the poet keep to the end of the poem the reason for his careering? Would the poem be as effective if this were revealed at the beginning?
- Does the poem read aloud well? Experiment with rewriting part of the poem as conventional verse. Where would the lines end? Does it still work as a poem? Does it work better as a shape poem? Why?
- Does the poem rhyme? Which words rhyme? Does it have a strong rhythm? How does the rhythm contribute to the effect of the poem?
- How does the poem make the children feel?

Focused word/sentence work

- Ask the children to pick out the expressive verbs of movement in the poem.
- Which other words and phrases are particularly effective? Why?

Independent work

- Children proofread and write final drafts of their shape poems from day 3. Those who have finished may write a second poem by choosing another idea from page 34 in the Pupil's Book, or developing one of their own.

Plenary

- Display and discuss more of the children's shape poems.

DAY 5

Big Book pp. 44–48; Pupil's Book p. 34

Shared reading

- Read again all the poems in the unit, together with the best of the children's own shape poems.
- How is the poem on page 48 similar to, or different from, those on pages 44–47.
- Which of all the poems in this unit do the children like best? Why?
- Which of the children's own poems is the class favourite? Discuss why this should be so.
- Which is most effective: what the poem has to say, its choice of words, its shape, or a combination of all three?

Focused word/sentence work

- Revise and consolidate, as necessary, appropriate word and sentence level objectives for this term, e.g. adding *-ing*, the spelling pattern *-le*, prefixes, synonyms, the purpose and organisation of a dictionary and thesaurus, punctuation (including speech marks) and verbs.

Independent work

- Children write more calligram sentences, using their own ideas or those given on page 34 in the Pupil's Book.

Plenary

- Display and discuss more of the children's own shape poems and calligram sentences.

Homework

- Page 11 in the Homework Book encourages the children to collect synonyms for ways of eating, drinking and cooking.

ASSESSMENT

Copymaster 10 is an assessment master of key word and sentence objectives for term 1, testing sentence construction and punctuation, speech marks, past tense and prefixes. Indirectly, it will also test vocabulary, spelling and handwriting. The completed sheet will be useful as a record of progress, together with examples of the pupils' text work.

TERM 2

HALF-TERMLY PLANNER

Year 3 • Term 2 • Weeks 1–5

SCHOOL _____ CLASS _____ TEACHER _____

		Phonetics, spelling and vocabulary	Grammar and punctuation	Comprehension and composition	Texts
Continuous work Weeks 1–5		WL 1, 2, 3, 4, 5, 6, 7, 17, 25, 26, 27	SL 1		**Range** **Fiction and poetry**: Myths, fables, traditional stories; stories with related themes **Non-fiction**: Instructions
Blocked work Week	Unit				**Titles**
1	11	WL 8, 9, 10, 16	SL 2, 4	TL 1, 2, 3, 6, 9	From *Aesop's Fables*, retold by Anne Gatti; From *Fables from Africa*, retold by Jan Knappert
2	12		SL 11	TL 1, 2, 3, 7	From *Turkish Folk-tales*, retold by Barbara K. Walker; From *The Three Little Pigs*, Joseph Jacobs
3	13	WL 9, 15	SL 4, 5, 6, 7, 8	TL 3, 6, 7, 8, 9, 10	From *Clever Polly and the Stupid Wolf*, Catherine Storr; From *Tales of Polly and the Hungry Wolf*, Catherine Storr
4	14		SL 2, 3, 9	TL 1, 2, 3, 6, 7, 9	From *Creation Stories*, retold by Maureen Stewart; From *Beginnings*, ed. P. Farmer
5	15		SL 10	TL 12, 13, 14, 15, 16, 17	From *Divali*, Howard Marsh; *Vanishing Colours* *A Plan of the Classroom*

TERM 2

HALF-TERMLY PLANNER

Year 3 • Term 2 • Weeks 6–10

SCHOOL _____   CLASS _____   TEACHER _____

		Phonetics, spelling and vocabulary	Grammar and punctuation	Comprehension and composition	Texts
Continuous work Weeks 6–10		WL 1, 2, 3, 4, 5, 6, 7, 17, 25, 26, 27	SL 1		**Range** **Fiction and poetry**: Myths, traditional stories; stories with related themes; oral and performance poetry **Non-fiction**: Dictionaries and thesauruses
Blocked work Week	Unit				**Titles**
6	16		SL 6, 7, 8, 10	TL 4, 5, 11, 12, 13, 14, 15, 16, 17	Games; *Skipping Rope Song*, Dionne Brand; *School Dinners*, Anon
7	17	WL 10, 19, 20, 21, 22, 23			From *Collins Primary Dictionary*; From *Collins Junior Thesaurus*; From *Collins Independent Dictionary*, Ginny Lapage
8	18	WL 18, 19, 24	SL 6, 9, 10	TL 1, 4, 5, 6, 7, 9	From *The Pied Piper of Hamelin*, Rose Impey; From *The Pied Piper of Hamelin*, Robert Browning
9	19	WL 9, 13, 14	SL 4, 5	TL 1, 10	From *The One-eyed Giant and Other Monsters from the Greek Myths*, Anne Rockwell; *Heracles*
10	20		SL 9, 10, 11	TL 1, 2, 6, 8, 9, 10	From *The Saga of Erik the Viking*, Terry Jones

Focus on Literacy Teacher's Resource Book 3 © Barry and Anita Scholes, HarperCollins*Publishers* Ltd 1999   41

Unit 11 Fables

Key Learning Objectives

TL1	To investigate the styles and voices of traditional story language
TL2	To identify typical story themes
TL3	To identify and discuss recurring characters, evaluate their behaviour and justify views
TL6	To plan main points as a structure for story writing
TL9	To write a story plan for own fable
SL2	To investigate the function of adjectives within sentences
SL4	To extend knowledge and understanding of pluralisation
WL8	To investigate how words change when *-er, -est* and *-y* are added
WL9	To investigate and identify basic rules for changing the spelling of nouns when *-s* is added
WL10	To use the terms "singular" and "plural" appropriately
WL16	To use the term "suffix"

Range:	Fables
Texts:	From *Aesop's Fables*, retold by Anne Gatti From *Fables From Africa*, retold by Jan Knappert
Resources:	Big Book 3B pp. 4–9 Pupil's Book 3 pp. 35–37 Homework Book 3 p.12: Suffixes: *-ness, -ly, -ful* Copymaster 11: Storyboard Copymaster 12: Fiction book review

DAY 1

Big Book pp. 4–7; Pupil's Book p. 36

Shared reading

- Read the fables to the children. Explain that a fable is a short story, often with animals as central characters, which teaches a moral lesson.
- Discuss similarities and differences between the fables.
- What is the theme of each story? Ask the children to explain the morals.
- Which stories have these typical themes: wise over foolish, weak over strong?

Focused word/sentence work

- Introduce and explain the terms "singular" and "plural".
- Investigate and identify some of the basic rules for changing the spelling of nouns when *-s* is added. Allow the pupils to discover these rules for themselves by asking them to pluralise nouns such as: *dog, crow, tree, fox, church, bush,* etc.
- Most nouns simply add *-s* without any changes. Words ending in *s, x, z, sh* or *ch* add *-es*, e.g. *bus – buses, fox – foxes, waltz – waltzes, brush – brushes, switch – switches.* These changes are explored further in the Pupil's Book.

Independent work

- Children answer the questions about the fables.

Plenary

- Review the children's independent text work, showing them how to find answers from the text.

DAY 2

Big Book pp. 4–7; Pupil's Book p. 36

Shared reading

- What do the children think of the behaviour of the animals? Encourage them to suggest suitable words to describe each animal.
- How is the dog in *The Greedy Dog* different from the one in *The Persistent Dog*?
- How is the ostrich similar to the crow?

Focused word/sentence work

- Introduce and explain the term *suffix*.
- Investigate words with the suffixes *-er* and *-ly*: big*ger* and larg*er* in *The Greedy Dog*.
- Allow the pupils to discover for themselves some of the rules for adding the suffixes *-er* and *-st*. Investigate the words *stronger, quicker, bigger, fatter,* etc. Page 36 in the Pupil's Book focuses on doubling the final consonant. It does not cover exceptions such as words ending in *w, x* or *y*, e.g. *fry – fryer*; where the consonant is preceded by two vowels, e.g. *creep – creeper*; or where there are two consonants, e.g. *fast – faster, turn – turner, search – searcher*. You may wish to explain these as the opportunity arises.
- Look for examples of verbs which do not add *-ed* to make the past tense, e.g. *stood, began, said, fell, saw, thought, swept, took, flew.*
- Revise the work from day 1 on pluralisation. Page 36 in the Pupil's Book explores the spelling pattern for pluralisation of nouns ending in the consonants *s, x, z, sh* and *ch* (adding *-es*).
- Discuss with the children the need for noun/verb agreement when rewriting some of the sentences in section B.

Independent work

- Children work on pluralisations on page 36 in the Pupil's Book.
- Children explore the use of the suffixes *-er, -est*.

Plenary

- Review the children's work on pluralising nouns.

DAY 3

Big Book pp. 4–7; Pupil's Book p. 37

Shared reading/writing, including focused word/sentence work

- Compare the beginnings and endings of the fables. In what ways are they similar?
- Prepare for story writing by asking the children to retell the stories in their own words.
- Page 37 in the Pupil's Book has ideas to help the children plan their own fable, using one of those in the Big Book as a model. Discuss ways of changing the fables, e.g. different characters or settings, while retaining the moral. A selection of animal characters is offered as ideas, together with three possible settings.
- Demonstrate how to plan the story using notes or a storyboard. Copymaster 11 will prove useful for this.

Independent work

- Children plan and write their own fable.

Plenary

- Review the children's work, offering help and encouragement.

DAY 4

Big Book pp. 4–9; Pupil's Book p. 37

Shared reading

- Read *The Lion's Share* on page 8 in the Big Book. What does the class think the moral is?
- What do the children think of the behaviour of the characters? In what way is the fox in this story similar to the fox in *The Foolish Crow*?
- Foxes and wolves are recurring characters in traditional tales. In what ways are they similar or different? Which seems to be the more cunning?

Focused word/sentence work

- Ask the children to pick out the adjectives in the stories. Experiment with deleting the adjectives. What effect does this have?
- Note the *-le* ending in the word *fable*.

Independent work

- Children continue with their fables. You may want those who have finished to choose a different fable as a model for a second story.
- The storyboard on Copymaster 11 may be used as a story planner, but it is also useful to help the children describe and sequence events from this or any other story.
- Copymaster 12 is a fiction book review focusing on character, and is equally suitable for this or any story.

Plenary

- Let the children read aloud their own fables. Compile the stories into a class big book.

DAY 5

Big Book pp. 8–9; Pupil's Book p. 37

Shared reading

- Ask the children to read the fable aloud.
- Discuss which of the fables in this unit the children like best, and which least. Ask them to justify their answers.
- Use the story for improvised drama.

Focused word/sentence work

- Note the word *mighty* formed by adding *-y* to the root word. Let the children discover the basic rules for adding *-y* from words such as *rain – rainy, ice – icy* and *sun – sunny*. These rules are: dropping a silent *e* before adding a suffix, and doubling the last consonant for short words ending in a consonant.

Independent work

- Children practise forming *-y* words on page 37 in the Pupil's Book.

Plenary

- Review the week's work, re-emphasising teaching points and clarifying misconceptions.

Consolidation and extension

- Let the children read aloud their favourite fable. Give them an opportunity to prepare the reading in advance.
- Copymaster 11 is a storyboard which may be used as a story planner, but it is also useful to help the children describe and sequence events from any story they have read.
- Copymaster 12 is a fiction book review focusing on character.

Homework

- Page 12 in the Homework Book gives practice in using the suffixes *-ly*, *-ness* and *-ful*.

Unit 12   Wolf Tales

Key Learning Objectives

TL1   To investigate the styles and voices of traditional story language

TL2   To identify typical story themes

TL3   To identify and discuss recurring characters, evaluate their behaviour and justify views

TL7   To describe and sequence key incidents

SL11 To understand the need for grammatical agreement

Range:	Traditional stories
Texts:	From *Turkish Folk-tales*, retold by Barbara K. Walker
	From *The Three Little Pigs*, Joseph Jacobs
Resources:	Big Book 3B pp. 10–13
	Pupil's Book 3 pp. 38–40
	Homework Book 3 p.13: Verb agreement: *am, is, are, was, were*
	Copymaster 13: Writing frame: a letter

DAY 1

Big Book pp. 10–11; Pupil's Book p. 39

Shared reading

- First read the story to the class, and then ask the children to read it aloud with a narrator and three others to read the dialogue of the wolf, rabbit and duck.
- The story is another example of a fable. Ask the children to identify its moral.
- Ask the class what the theme of the story is: wise over foolish. It may also be said to show the triumph of good over evil.
- Ask the children to retell the story in their own words. Structure this into beginning, middle and end, helping them to identify significant events in each part of the story. The children may need support in understanding what a significant event is.

Focused word/sentence work

- Identify the adjectives in the passage, e.g. *great, big, fat, cruel*.
- Discuss what they all have in common: they qualify, or describe, nouns.
- Ask the children to match adjectives to the nouns they describe.

Independent work

- Page 39 in the Pupil's Book gives practice in sequencing key events in the story. The beginning, middle and ending of the story are illustrated to help the children.
- Copymaster 11 may be used to storyboard the fable, with the sentences from the book as captions, or the children might write their own.

Plenary

- Review the children's independent text work.

DAY 2

Big Book pp. 10–11; Pupil's Book p. 39

Shared reading

- Investigate the way this story opens and closes. Compare it with the beginnings and endings of the fables in Unit 11.
- Encourage the children to collect examples of traditional story openings and endings, continuing their collection throughout the term. These may be entered in a computer database, linking with information technology. From time to time you may wish to discuss these examples and identify recurring language.
- What other stories do the children know which have the recurring character of the wolf? How does the wolf behave in these stories? How would the children respond to him? Ask them to justify their views.
- Investigate the style and voice of this fable. Look at the opening and ending. Note the sentence which announces a scene change: "So both of them went to the duck."

Focused word/sentence work

- Remind the children what a comma is. Ask them to look for commas in the text. Discuss how they help the reader. Demonstrate this by reading the text aloud.
- Discuss the need for grammatical agreement. Focus on the verb *to be*. Why is it right to say a rabbit *was* walking in the forest, but not a rabbit *were* walking? What are the present tense equivalents of *was* and *were*?
- Ask the children to make up sentences using *is, are, was* and *were*.

Independent work

- Page 39 in the Pupil's Book offers consolidation of the children's understanding of the need for grammatical agreement with the verb *to be*.

Plenary

- Review the children's work on verb agreement. Clarify any misconceptions.

DAY 3

Big Book pp. 10–11; Pupil's Book p. 40

Shared reading/writing

- Discuss the behaviour of the three characters in *The Rabbit and the Wolf*. What do the children think about them? Ask them to justify their views.
- Ask the children to retell the story from the different points of view of the three characters.
- Discuss what the rabbit might say about the incident in a letter to a friend. Write the letter together. As you do so, draw attention to how letters are set out.

Focused word/sentence work

- Investigate the words in the text with silent letters: *walking, caught, listened, thought, wrong*.

- Ask the children to use the "look, say, cover, write, check" strategy to learn to spell these words.

Independent work

- The children write their own letters in the role of the rabbit.
- Copymaster 13 offers a writing frame for this activity.

Plenary

- Review the work in progress, providing feedback and encouragement to pupils.

DAY 4
Big Book pp. 12–13; Pupil's Book p. 40

Shared reading

- Read the extract from *The Three Little Pigs*. How are the wolves similar in these stories?
- Is this story a fable? What makes the children think so? What kind of story is it? How can the class tell?
- Look at the use of repetition. What does this tell us about who the story is intended for?
- Do the children know any other versions of this story? In what ways are they different? Why should this be so?

Focused word/sentence work

- Explore the use of commas, reading the text aloud to show their purpose in helping the reader.

Independent work

- Children continue their letters from day 3.
- Those who have finished might write a letter from the wolf to one of his friends, giving his view on the events. Alternatively some children may prefer to write a letter to the wolf complaining about his bad behaviour, and explaining why he should mend his ways.

Plenary

- Ask the children to read their letters aloud.

DAY 5
Big Book pp. 12–13; Pupil's Book p. 40

Shared reading

- Ask the children to read the story aloud, with different children taking the parts of the wolf, the pig and the narrator. Encourage them to use the punctuation to help them.
- Ask them to retell the entire story, including what happened to the first two pigs in this well-known story.

Focused word/sentence work

- Investigate the words in the passage with silent letters: *knocked*, *climb*, *through*.
- Revise the work on agreement with the verb *to be*, with particular emphasis on *I am* and *we are*.

Independent work

- Children revise and consolidate verb agreement on page 40 in the Pupil's Book. This activity includes work on *am*, *is*, *are*, *was* and *were*.

Plenary

- Review the week's work, re-emphasising teaching points and clarifying misconceptions.

Consolidation and extension

- Encourage the children to write what might happen to the wolf after the duck and rabbit have left him with the stone on his back. Will he have learned a lesson?
- Copymaster 13 is a writing frame for letter writing.

Homework

- Page 13 in the Homework Book consolidates work on pronoun/verb agreement.

Unit 13 Polly and the Wolf

Key Learning Objectives

TL3	To identify and discuss recurring characters, evaluate their behaviour and justify views
TL6	To plan main points as a structure for story writing
TL7	To describe and sequence key incidents
TL8	To write portraits of characters, using story text to describe behaviour and characteristics
TL9	To write a story plan for own traditional tale
TL10	To write alternative sequels to traditional stories using same characters and settings
SL4	To extend knowledge and understanding of pluralisation
SL5	To use the terms "singular" and "plural" appropriately
SL6	To note where commas occur in reading and to discuss their functions in helping the reader
SL7	To use the term "comma" appropriately in relation to reading
SL8	To be aware of other uses of capitalisation from reading
WL9	To investigate and identify basic rules for changing the spelling of nouns when -s is added
WL15	To use the apostrophe to spell shortened forms of words

Range:	Stories with themes related to traditional stories
Texts:	From *Clever Polly and the Stupid Wolf*, Catherine Storr From *Tales of Polly and the Hungry Wolf*, Catherine Storr
Resources:	Big Book 3B pp. 14–19 Pupil's Book 3 pp. 41–43 Homework Book 3 p. 14: Punctuation Copymaster 14: Planning a story Copymaster 15: Book review: a story

DAY 1

Big Book pp. 14–16; Pupil's Book p. 42

Shared reading

- In what ways is the story different from *The Rabbit and the Wolf*?
- In what ways is it similar to *The Rabbit and the Wolf*? Does it have a similar theme?
- Examine the opening sentence to the story. Compare it to the opening sentence of *The Rabbit and the Wolf*. Ask the children to find the sentence which is the scene opener for the wolf's second visit. How is this similar to, or different from, the opening sentence?
- What do the children think of Polly? Would they have reacted in the same way? Ask them to justify their response.
- Ask the children to describe and sequence the key incidents in the story.

Focused word/sentence work

- Ask the children to look for examples of compound words, e.g. *upstairs, downstairs, another*. From which shorter words are they made?
- Ask the children to pick out examples of nouns from the passage. Make a list of the words they suggest. Try pluralisation as a test for identifying nouns. Ask the children to change the list of nouns into plurals.

Independent work

- Children copy and complete a chart which sequences the key incidents in the story.
- Children predict what might happen when the wolf returns.

Plenary

- Review the children's independent text work.

DAY 2

Big Book pp. 14–16; Pupil's Book p. 42

Shared reading

- Compare the way the wolf is tricked in this story to *The Rabbit and the Wolf*. How are the two wolves similar? Let the children suggest adjectives to describe the wolf.
- Ask the children to prepare for reading the text aloud with appropriate intonation and expression. Choose a narrator and two children to read the dialogue of Polly and the wolf.
- Look at the use of commas in the text and encourage the children to use these to help them in their reading aloud.

Focused word/sentence work

- Investigate the apostrophe in shortened forms of words, e.g. *I'm, don't, haven't*. Explain that the apostrophe stands for a missing letter or letters. Help the children distinguish between an apostrophe and a comma.
- Revise the basic rules for pluralisation: adding -s as in *doors, bells*, and changing -f to -ves as in *wolves*. Note the exceptions to the rule about nouns ending in -f: *chief, roof, cliff* and *staff* all just add -s. A few words have two acceptable endings for plurals, e.g. *dwarfs* or *dwarves*, *handkerchiefs* or *handkerchieves*, *hoofs* or *hooves*, *scarfs* or *scarves*.
- Point out that not all nouns can be made plural: e.g. *sheep* remains unchanged in its plural form, words such as *vermin* are always plural, and some nouns are collective, e.g. *herd, swarm*, etc.

Independent work

- Children to put into practice their understanding of the apostrophe in shorter forms.
- The second activity on page 42 in the Pupil's Book focuses on spelling patterns for pluralisation of nouns.

Plenary

- Review the children's work on the apostrophe in shorter forms. Clarify any misconceptions.
- Revise and practise the spelling rules for pluralisation of nouns ending in -f.

46

DAY 3

Big Book pp. 14–16; Pupil's Book p. 43

Shared writing

- Read the story of Polly and the wolf again. Ask the children to describe the key incidents for the beginning, middle and end of the story.
- Discuss other aspects of the story: the setting, the opening sentence.
- Talk about other ways in which the wolf might try to catch Polly. How might Polly avoid his trickery?
- Choose the best of the children's ideas and plan a story together, using the framework on page 43 in the Pupil's Book.
- Encourage the children to identify typical phrases and expressions from the original story to help them structure the writing.
- Discuss different ways of adapting Catherine Storr's opening sentence as the first sentence of the shared writing.

Focused word/sentence work

- Prepare for the children's own story writing by revising verb tense. Look for examples of adding *-ed*, e.g. *watered, asked*. Most of the other past tense verbs in the passage are irregular examples, e.g. *went, said, led, ran, ate, slunk*. Some of the verbs do not change when forming the past tense, e.g. *put, cut*.

Independent work

- Children write their own sequel to the Polly and the wolf adventure. Copymaster 14 is a story planner to help with this work.

Plenary

- Review the work in progress, offering advice and encouragement. Draw attention to good practice.

DAY 4

Big Book pp. 17–19; Pupil's Book p. 43

Shared reading

- Read the opening to the later Polly and the wolf story *The Spell*. Has the wolf changed from the first story? Is his new idea a sensible one? Ask the children to justify their answers.
- Compare the opening sentence with the earlier extract, and those of the stories in Units 11 and 12. How is it different from those traditional stories?
- How does the class think the wolf will find a spell? What might happen when he tries to use it?

Focused word/sentence work

- Ask the children to pick out the adjectives in the text, e.g. *loud, stupid, little, beautiful, handsome, several, small, juicy, unpleasant*. Which nouns do they describe?
- Experiment with deleting these adjectives. What effect does this have on the meaning? Substitute different adjectives, and discuss their effect on meaning.

Independent work

- Children continue their sequels.

Plenary

- Ask the children to read aloud their sequels to the Polly and the wolf story.

DAY 5

Big Book pp. 17–19; Pupil's Book p. 43

Shared reading

- What kind of book has given the wolf his idea for a spell? Which words and phrases give clues?
- Encourage the children to suggest stories they know which might have been in the wolf's book, e.g. *The Frog Prince*. Ask them to retell one of these stories, describing the key incidents.
- Ask the children to read the extract aloud, using the punctuation, especially commas, to help them.

Focused word/sentence work

- Notice the use of capital letters for the title, Polly's name and the beginnings of sentences.
- Investigate the use of punctuation marks: full stops, question and exclamation marks, commas and speech marks.

Independent work

- Children revise and consolidate their understanding of punctuation, using page 43 in the Pupil's Book.

Plenary

- Review the week's work, re-emphasising teaching points and clarifying misconceptions.

Consolidation and extension

- Encourage the children to explore the character of the wolf by designing a Wanted poster.
- Encourage the children to continue collecting opening sentences from their reading, using Copymaster 1.
- Copymaster 14 is a story planner which focuses on character, setting and plot.
- Copymaster 15 is a book review for a story. This follows a similar format to the story planner on Copymaster 14, to help the children appreciate that all stories have similar features: a setting, characters, a beginning, middle and end. The importance of the opening sentence is also stressed.

Homework

- Page 14 in the Homework Book focuses on the use of capital letters in names and book titles.

Unit 14: The Birth of the Sun

Key Learning Objectives

TL1	To investigate the styles and voices of traditional story language
TL2	To identify typical story themes
TL3	To identify and discuss recurring characters, evaluate their behaviour and justify views
TL6	To plan main points as a structure for story writing
TL7	To describe and sequence key incidents
TL9	To write a story plan for own myth
SL2	To investigate the function of adjectives within sentences
SL3	To use the term "adjective" appropriately
SL9	To experiment with deleting words in sentences to see which are essential to meaning and which are not

Range:	Creation myths
Texts:	From *Creation Stories*, retold by Maureen Stewart
	From *Beginnings*, ed. P. Farmer
Resources:	Big Book 3B pp. 20–23
	Pupil's Book 3 pp. 44–46
	Homework Book 3 p.15: More about adjectives

DAY 1

Big Book pp. 20–21; Pupil's Book p. 45

Shared reading

- This story is an Aborigine myth. Explain that the Aborigines are the original inhabitants of Australia.
- A myth is a story which explains natural phenomena, using supernatural characters.
- Read the story to the children. Encourage them to use their awareness of grammar to decipher new or unfamiliar words, or to infer meaning from context.
- Ask the children to retell the story in their own words, identifying the beginning of the story, the middle and the end. What is the theme of the story? Who are the supernatural characters?

Focused word/sentence work

- Investigate the words in the text with silent letters: *light, thought, could, laughter*.
- Ask the children to think of opposites for some of the adjectives in the text: *young, dim, angry, bright, dry, cloudy, strong, loud*. Ask them to use these opposites in sentences of their own.

Independent work

- Children sequence sentences about the story. To help them, the sentences are listed under the headings: beginning, middle and ending.

Plenary

- Review the children's independent work.
- Ask the children to retell the story in their own words.

DAY 2

Big Book pp. 20–21; Pupil's Book p. 45

Shared reading

- Read the story again.
- Do the children think this is a satisfying explanation of the creation of the sun? Can the children suggest what this myth does not explain about the sun (e.g. its movement across the sky, its varying intensity in summer and winter)?
- Investigate the styles and voices of traditional story language in this myth, e.g. "When the world was very young ...", "Then came a time ..." etc.
- Do the children know any other creation myths, or modern stories which explain things (e.g. the *How the Whale Became* stories by Ted Hughes)?

Focused word/sentence work

- Ask the children to pick out adjectives in the story, e.g. *young, dim, bright, yellow, cloudy*. Which nouns do they describe? (Note that "young" and "cloudy" do not precede the nouns.) Investigate the effect of deleting these adjectives, e.g. "The yolk of the egg burst into a flame." How does this change the meaning? What happens when "young" is deleted? Does the text still make sense? How important are adjectives in helping us to imagine things?
- Note the use of the noun "morning" as an adjective – "the *morning* star". Can the children suggest other uses of this word as an adjective (e.g. *morning paper, train, lessons*)? Can they suggest other nouns which may be used as adjectives?

Independent work

- Children work on classifying adjectives into colour, shape, size and mood on page 45 in the Pupil's Book.

Plenary

- Review the children's classification of adjectives. Discuss further adjectives which might be added to their lists.

DAY 3

Big Book pp. 20–21; Pupil's Book p. 46

Shared writing, including focused word/sentence work

- Read *The Birth of the Sun* again.
- Discuss with the children the ideas on page 46 in the Pupil's Book for a creation myth of their own.
- Select one of these ideas and make notes of the children's suggestions for developing it.
- Plan the story together. Consider setting, characters, beginning, middle and end, and the opening sentence.

- Investigate how the opening sentence from *The Birth of the Sun* might be adapted to your story. Look for other styles and voices of creation myths which might be included, e.g. "Then came a time ...", "At first ...", "Later on ...", etc.

Independent work

- Children plan and write a myth of their own choosing or work independently on the shared plan.
- Copymaster 14 will be useful as a planning sheet.

Plenary

- Review the writing in progress, offering help and encouragement.

DAY 4
Big Book pp. 22–23; Pupil's Book p. 46

Shared reading

- The creation myth on page 22 of the Big Book is from North Borneo. Ask the children to describe and sequence the main points.
- Investigate the style and voice of this myth, picking out examples, e.g. "There was nothing but sea", "After a while ...", "In a little while longer still ...", etc.

Focused word/sentence work

- Investigate the verbs in the text, exploring those which do not simply add -ed to make the past tense: *fell*, *bred*, *grew*. Notice that *spread* does not change.
- Ask the children to use these verbs in sentences of their own.

Independent work

- Children continue work on their creation myth.

Plenary

- Review the writing in progress. Read particularly good examples to the class.

DAY 5
Big Book pp. 20–23; Pupil's Book p. 46

Shared reading/writing

- In what ways is the story of *The First People* similar to *The Birth of the Sun*? In what ways is it different?
- Revise the key incidents in the story. Make a list of them.
- Ask the children to retell the story in their own words.

Focused word/sentence work

- Pick out the adjectives from the text, e.g. *deep*, *tall*, *shady*. Ask the children to use these in sentences of their own.

Independent work

- Ask those who have not finished their creation myth to continue.
- Children practise and consolidate their understanding of adjectives on page 46 in the Pupil's Book.

Plenary

- Discuss the children's choice of adjectives and opposites from their independent work.

Consolidation and extension

- Read together, and discuss, the children's stories.
- Divide the children into ten small groups to work on one incident each in the creation of the earth story, e.g. the sky arched over the earth; a rock fell down from the sky into the water; slime covered the rock, etc. Ask each group to work to produce a picture with a caption for that part of the story.
- Ask the children to sequence their finished work. Display the picture story.
- You may later use the stories to compile a big book, either as a class book with illustrations, or as an audio cassette.

Homework

- Page 15 in the Homework Book has further practice in using adjectives.

Unit 15 Instructions

Key Learning Objectives

TL12 To identify the different purposes of instructional texts

TL13 To discuss the merits and limitations of particular instructional texts

TL14 To become familiar with how instructions are organised

TL15 To read and follow simple instructions

TL16 To write instructions

TL17 To make clear notes

SL10 To understand the differences between verbs in the 1st, 2nd and 3rd person

Range:	Instructions
Texts:	From *Divali* by Howard Marsh *Vanishing Colours* *Plan of a Classroom*
Resources:	Big Book 3B pp. 24–27 Pupil's Book 3 pp. 47–49 Homework Book 3 p. 16: Word building Copymaster 16: Making notes Copymaster 17: Writing frame: a recipe

Preparation

- Although it is not essential to actually make the chocolate coconut balls or the colour wheel as decribed in this unit, following the instructions will greatly facilitate achievement of the learning objectives.
- For the recipe you will need:
  225g desiccated coconut
  100g icing sugar
  1 small can condensed milk (200g)
  250g block of cooking chocolate, for coating
  waxed paper on which to set finished sweets (paper from a cornflakes packet is ideal)
  a small basin
  a pan and cooker for simmering the water
- For the colour wheel you will need: card, protractor, crayons, a piece of dowling about 15cm long, scissors.
- It would also be useful to make available examples of other instructional texts for comparison purposes, and to widen the children's experience of such texts.

DAY 1

Big Book pp. 24–27; Pupil's Book p. 48

Shared reading

- What kind of instructions are there in Unit 15? Discuss their purpose. Emphasise why they need to be clear, complete and in the correct sequence. What other kinds of instructions can the children think of, e.g. rules for games, bus timetables, routefinders, plans. Discuss their purpose. Ask the children to collect examples of as many kinds as they can.
- Examine how recipes and instructions are organised, e.g. a list of ingredients or materials, numbered steps and pictures.

Focused word/sentence work

- Investigate the conciseness of instructions: how they concentrate on the important words. Why are concise instructions easier to read and follow?
- Explain that some words are more essential to meaning than others. These are the key words. Short, unimportant words such as *a*, *the* and *and* may usually be left out without affecting the sense of the passage. Ask the children to pick out the key words in the text.
- Show how the key words can then be written as notes, using punctuation marks such as commas and dashes to make things clear.

Independent work

- Children complete a flow diagram based on the numbered steps in the chocolate coconut balls recipe.
- Children make notes on the same recipe.

Plenary

- Ask some children to read their notes to the class.
- Allow time for the children to reflect upon what they have learned in making notes, and to clarify their thinking.

DAY 2

Big Book pp. 24–26; Pupil's Book p. 48

Shared reading

- Let the children read and follow the instructions for making the chocolate coconut balls or the colour wheel. How easy are the instructions to follow? Is there anything that needs to be clearer? Stress the need for safety precautions.

Focused word/sentence work

- Explain the differences between first, second and third person accounts. Notice that the word *you* is usually left out in second person accounts: *colour the segments* is the same as *you colour the segments*.
- Compare instructions written in the second person with narratives written in the third person.
- Discuss the purposes for which each is used: first person for diaries, personal letters, second person for instructions, and third person for narratives and recounts.
- Experiment with transforming some of the instructions into the third person as a report. Draw attention to the words that need changing.

Independent work

- Children explore changing verbs to a different person.

Plenary

- Consolidate teaching points on the first, second and third person.

DAY 3

Big Book pp. 24–26; Pupil's Book p. 49

Shared reading/writing and focused word/sentence work

- Compare the recipe and instructions for making the colour wheel. How are they similar? How are they different?
- Examine the use of the present tense in instructions. Why should they be written in this way? How is this different from a report?
- Nouns and verbs are usually predominant in instructions. Highlight these to show how instructions differ from narratives. Compare the instructions with *The Birth of the Sun* in Unit 14.
- Page 49 in the Pupil's Book offers a choice of writing instructions for simple tasks. Select one of these to work through with the class. Emphasise the use of the present tense and second person, and the need for clear, concise instructions.

Independent work

- Children write instructions for one of the listed activities.
- Ask the children to check the clarity of their instructions, and then to exchange them with a classmate as a further check on clarity.

Plenary

- How might the instructions be improved?

DAY 4

Big Book p. 27; Pupil's Book p. 49

Shared reading

- Look at the plan of the classroom. What is the purpose of the key? Use the key to identify all the features of the plan.
- Ask the children the questions in *To think and talk about*.

Focused word/sentence work

- Ask the children to make up definitions for common classroom items, e.g. *blackboard, litter bin, cupboard*. Aim for precision and accuracy.
- Encourage the children to evaluate their definitions.

Independent work

- The second writing activity on page 49 in the Pupil's Book helps the children structure their own recipe. Copymaster 17 is a writing frame for this activity.
- Encourage them to check their work carefully to make sure they have left nothing out, and that everything is clear and in the right order.

Plenary

- Ask the children to evaluate their instructions, commenting on each other's work. Discuss what changes might be made and why they are necessary.

DAY 5

Big Book p. 27; Pupil's Book p. 49

Shared reading

- Ask the children to give directions from one place on the plan to another.
- Do the same for places in your own classroom.

Focused word/sentence work

- Ask the children to pick out the compound words in the text: *classroom, bookshelf, cupboard, blackboard*.
- Ask the children to make or suggest more compound words.

Independent work

- Children work on compound words on page 49 in the Pupil's Book.

Plenary

- Review the week's work, consolidating teaching points.

Consolidation and extension

- Give further practice in following instructions in other curriculum areas such as science.
- Make a plan of your own classroom.
- Compile the children's recipes into a class recipe book with contents page and index.
- Copymaster 16 has the text of the colour wheel instructions for the children to highlight the key words, and then rewrite as notes.
- Copymaster 17 is a writing frame for any recipe.

Homework

- Page 16 in the Homework Book focuses on building compound words and using them in sentences.

Unit 16: Games

Key Learning Objectives

TL4	To prepare poems for performance
TL5	To rehearse and improve performance
TL11	To write new or extended verses for performance based on models
TL12	To identify the different purposes of instructional texts
TL13	To discuss the merits and limitations of particular instructional texts
TL14	To become familiar with how instructions are organised
TL15	To read and follow simple instructions
TL16	To write instructions
TL17	To make clear notes
SL6	To note where commas occur in reading and to discuss their functions in helping the reader
SL7	To use the term "comma" appropriately in relation to reading
SL8	To be aware of other uses of capitalisation from reading
SL10	To understand the differences between verbs in the 1st, 2nd and 3rd person

Range:	Instructions; oral poetry
Texts:	*Achi* *Nine Men's Morris* *School Dinners*, Anon; *Skipping Rope Song*, Dionne Brand, from *A Caribbean Dozen*, ed. John Agard and Grace Nichols
Resources:	Big Book 3B pp. 28–31 Pupil's Book 3 pp. 50–52 Homework Book 3 p. 17: Word fun Copymaster 18: Game boards for Achi and Nine Men's Morris Copymaster 19: Writing frame: rules for a board game

DAY 1

Big Book pp. 28–29; Pupil's Book p. 51

Shared reading

- Identify the purpose of rules for games. What sort of things do they need to tell us?
- Read the rules for the board game Achi. Examine how they are organised, e.g. list of equipment, numbered points, list of correctly sequenced instructions.
- Discuss the words which "signpost", e.g. *when ..., once ..., each time ...*
- Ask the children questions about the game, e.g. Where did it originate? How many players? What is the aim of the game?
- Let the children play the game. You will need four counters per person. The game boards for both Achi and Nine Men's Morris are reproduced on Copymaster 18. You may prefer to enlarge these to A3 when copying.

Focused word/sentence work

- A *morris* is an old dance. Why is Nine Men's Morris so called?
- Notice that instructions are given in the present tense.
- Practise picking out the key words in the instructions for Achi. Write them as notes.

Independent work

- Children answer questions about the games.

Plenary

- Review the children's independent work.

DAY 2

Big Book pp. 28–29; Pupil's Book p. 51

Shared reading

- Read the rules for Nine Men's Morris. How are these similar to or different from those for Achi? How many players can play it? What is the aim of the game?
- Let the children read and follow the instructions to play Nine Men's Morris.
- After playing the two games, discuss which the children enjoyed most and why. Which was easier to play? Were the instructions clear?

Focused word/sentence work

- Explain the use of the homophones *to*, *too* and *two*. Ask the children to give examples of their correct use in sentences.

Independent work

- Page 51 in the Pupil's Book focuses on the homophones *to*, *too* and *two*. This is followed by a spelling activity: replacing missing letters in words. Clues are given to help identify the word.
- Other activities on page 51 in the Pupil's Book are finding missing letters and word pairs.

Plenary

- Discuss the children's independent work.

DAY 3

Big Book pp. 28–29; Pupil's Book p. 52

Shared writing and focused word/sentence work

- Read again the instructions for the games in this unit. Note particularly how the instructions are presented: headings, sequencing and the use of "signpost" words, e.g. *when ..., once ..., the winner is ...*
- Investigate the use of capital letters in the texts: headings, proper nouns.
- Page 52 in the Pupil's Book includes a planner for writing rules for a board game of the children's choice. Select one of the children's suggestions for a game. This should also be one you know well.

- Use the headings given to make notes on the game.
- Write full instructions for an audience who knows nothing at all about the game. Read aloud each instruction as it is written. Ask the children if it is clear. Have you missed anything out? Can the instruction be made more concise?
- Copymaster 19 is a writing frame for this activity.

Independent work
- Children write their own instructions for a board game of their choice.

Plenary
- Review work in progress, with specific reference to layout, sequencing and clarity.

DAY 4
Big Book pp. 30–31; Pupil's Book p. 52

Shared reading
- Read the two rhymes on pages 30–31 of the Big Book. Ask the children to tap out the rhythm of the *Skipping Rope Song* as you read. Why does this poem have a strong rhythm?
- Do the same with *School Dinners*. Does this rhyme have a strong rhythm? Does it need a strong rhythm? Compare the purposes of the two rhymes.
- Investigate the words in the poems which rhyme. Which words are half rhymes (e.g. *steel* and *will*, *better* and *pepper*)?

Focused word/sentence work
- Investigate the use of capital letters in these verses. Most poems begin each line with a capital letter. Which poem does not entirely follow this rule?
- Look at the use of commas in these verses, e.g. at the end of lines, in a list.

Independent work
- Children continue their work on the board game instructions.
- Alternatively, ask the children to write their own skipping rhyme, or a new verse about school dinners, using those verses as models.

Plenary
- Evaluate the children's instructions. Are the instructions correctly sequenced? Is the "signposting" clear?

DAY 5
Big Book pp. 30–31; Pupil's Book p. 52

Shared reading
- Ask the children to read the playground rhymes aloud, taking note of punctuation and meaning.
- What other playground rhymes do the children know? Ask them to recite them and explain their purpose.
- Ask those children who have written their own playground rhymes to read them aloud.
- Begin a class big book of playground chants and rhymes.

Focused word/sentence work
- Explore the use of the apostrophe in short forms: *didn't*, *don't*, *'cause*.

Independent work
- Page 52 in the Pupil's Book has a number of word puzzle activities for the children to enjoy.

Plenary
- Review the week's work.
- Evaluate the children's board game instructions.

Consolidation and extension

- Ask the children to prepare playground rhymes for performance. Allow them time to rehearse and improve their performance.
- Copymaster 18 has game boards for Achi and Nine Men's Morris.
- Copymaster 19 is a writing frame for board game rules.

Homework

- Page 17 in the Homework Book has further word fun activities: a word step crossword and animal anagrams.

Unit 17 The Meaning of Words

Key Learning Objectives

WL10 To investigate, spell and read words with silent letters

WL19 To use dictionaries to learn or check the spellings and definitions of words

WL20 To write their own definitions of words, developing precision and accuracy in expression

WL21 To use the term "definition"

WL22 To know the quartiles of the dictionary

WL23 To organise words or information alphabetically, using the first two letters

Range:	Dictionaries, thesauruses
Texts:	From *Collins Primary Dictionary*
	From *Collins Junior Thesaurus*
	From *Collins Independent Dictionary*, Ginny Lapage
Resources:	Big Book 3B pp. 32–35
	Pupil's Book 3 pp. 53–55
	Homework Book 3 p. 18: Silent letters

Preparation

- Make available dictionaries and thesauruses, preferably *Collins Primary Dictionary* or *Collins Independent Dictionary*, and *Collins Junior Thesaurus*.

- There is no shared writing in this unit, as the time is devoted to exploring how to use the quartiles of a dictionary to find words quickly, to encourage children to write their own definitions of words and to check these with a dictionary.

DAY 1

Big Book p. 32; Pupil's Book p. 54

Shared reading

- Discuss the purpose of a dictionary. In what ways is it a useful book?

- Look at how the words in a dictionary are organised in alphabetical order: all the *A* words grouped together, etc. How are words beginning with the same letter organised?

- Introduce the term "definition". Investigate how dictionaries give definitions. Why do some words have more than one definition? Why does the word *nearly* have an example to show how it is used? Why are *-er* and *-est* forms given for the words *narrow*, *nasty* and *naughty*? What kind of words are these?

Focused word/sentence work

- Ask the children to find words on the dictionary page which are nouns. How can they tell? Use the pluralisation test and discuss the results.

- Revise the alphabet. Explain how to organise words alphabetically, using the first two letters. Give practice with suitable words.

Independent work

- Children use the dictionary and thesaurus extracts to explore words.

Plenary

- Review the children's independent work.

DAY 2

Big Book p. 33; Pupil's Book p. 54

Shared reading

- Introduce the word *synonym*. Examine the extract from the thesaurus and how it is organised. Why are the words listed in six different boxes? How is the sixth box different? Look at the words in the first box and the example. Could the other words in the list be substituted for *gentle*? Could *silent, restful, still* or *shy* be substituted instead? Ask the children to justify their response. Do all the synonyms for *quiet* have exactly the same meaning? How many synonyms for *loud* can the children find?

Focused word/sentence work

- Make thesauruses available to the children. Practise finding suitable synonyms for common words.

- Ask the children to use the synonyms they find, in sentences of their own.

Independent work

- Page 54 in the Pupil's Book gives practice in alphabetical order using the first two letters, and in using words in sentences to show their meaning.

- Encourage the children to use the "look, say, cover, write, check" strategy to learn some of the words listed in section A.

- The second activity on page 54 in the Pupil's Book explores synonyms by asking the children to find synonyms for a number of common words. Encourage them first to think of synonyms from their own experience or from reading. They may then extend their lists using a thesaurus.

Plenary

- Revise and practise alphabetical order to the second letter.

- Ask the children to give synonyms for *big, small, angry, frightened,* and/or others.

DAY 3

Pupil's Book p. 55

Shared reading, including focused word/sentence work

- Ask the children to open the dictionary at a point half way through. Write down the first letter of the words they find there. Do the same at the quarter and three-quarter marks. Make a list of the initial letters of words which may be found in each quartile. Demonstrate how this knowledge is useful in opening the dictionary to approximately the right place, thus saving valuable time.

- Once the correct initial letter has been found, show how to find a particular word using alphabetisation to the second letter.
- Give practice in finding words quickly using this knowledge.
- Extend this by asking for the definition of the word, and then asking for the word to be used in a sentence to show its meaning.

Independent work

- Page 55 in the Pupil's Book has a list of words to consolidate knowledge of dictionary quartiles.
- Children use a dictionary to find the answers to the questions in the *Finding out* section.

Plenary

- Ask the children in turn to challenge the rest of the class to find words in the dictionary as quickly as they can. Ensure that they have first checked that the suggested word is listed in the particular dictionary the class is using.

DAY 4
Big Book pp. 32, 34; Pupil's Book p. 55

Shared reading, including focused word/sentence work

- Compare the extract from *Collins Independent Dictionary* on page 34 of the Big Book with the extract on page 32. How is it different? What extra information does it give (parts of speech, plurals and verb endings)? How useful is this extra information?
- Close the book and ask the children to make up their own definition for a word listed in the dictionary extract, e.g. *poor, pool, port, post* (as a verb and a noun), *popular* or *pond*. Compare the children's definitions with those in the dictionary. Why is it important to have a precise definition of a word?
- Give the children practice in making up their own definitions for other common words, and then checking them in a dictionary. Ask the children to suggest ways of making their own definitions more precise, or concise.

Independent work

- Children write their own definitions for familiar words and check them with a dictionary.

Plenary

- Revise and consolidate the work by asking the children to give their own definitions for *table, February, jelly, house, rain* and/or others. Check them against a dictionary for preciseness.

DAY 5
Big Book pp. 32–35; Pupil's Book p. 55

Shared reading

- Discuss the different uses of a dictionary and thesaurus.
- How useful is a dictionary for checking spellings? What happens if you are not sure what letter the word begins with? This may happen with words which sound as if they begin with a different letter, e.g. *photograph, character, cereal, xylophone*. It may also happen with silent letters, e.g. *gnome, wrong, knot*. There is a useful guide to tracking down words such as these at the front of *Collins Junior Thesaurus*.

Focused word/sentence work

- Make a shared list of words with silent letters. Discuss spelling strategies for them.

Independent work

- Children explore silent letters on page 55 of the Pupil's Book.

Plenary

- Revise and consolidate using a dictionary and thesaurus, with particular reference to alphabetical order, definitions, dictionary quartiles and synonyms.

Consolidation and extension

- Encourage the children to make their own dictionaries of special words: those linked to particular topics or themes, personal or significant words derived from own reading or which relate to their own lives. Make alphabetical lists together of words that might be included.

Homework

- Page 18 in the Homework Book consolidates work on silent letters, and encourages the "look, say, cover, write, check" strategy of learning spellings.

Unit 18   Rats!

Key Learning Objectives

TL1   To investigate the styles and voices of traditional story language

TL4   To prepare poems for performance

TL5   To rehearse and improve performance

TL6   To plan main points as a structure for story writing

TL7   To describe and sequence key incidents

TL9   To write a story plan for own traditional tale

SL6   To note where commas occur in reading and to discuss their functions in helping the reader

SL9   To experiment with deleting words in sentences to see which are essential to meaning and which are not

SL10   To understand the differences between verbs in the 1st, 2nd and 3rd person

WL18   To infer the meaning of unknown words from context and generate a range of possible meanings

WL19   To use dictionaries to learn or check the spellings and definitions of words

WL24   To explore opposites

Range:	Traditional story Poem for performance
Texts:	From *The Pied Piper of Hamelin*, Rose Impey From *The Pied Piper of Hamelin*, Robert Browning
Resources:	Big Book 3B pp. 36–39 Pupil's Book 3 pp. 56–58 Homework Book 3 p. 19: Opposites

Preparation

- Find a copy of the full story of *The Pied Piper* to read to the children outside the literacy hour. This will be a useful resource for the shared writing on day 3.
- Make dictionaries available for day 2, preferably *Collins Primary Dictionary*.

DAY 1

Big Book pp. 36–37; Pupil's Book p. 57

Shared reading

- Read the story to the children. Most may know how the story continues. Ask them to re-tell the rest of the story. What is the theme of the story?
- Ask the children to identify the main idea for each paragraph.

Focused word/sentence work

- Investigate the changes made when *-er* is added to *thin* and *fat*.
- Experiment with changing plural sentences to singular. Discuss the words which have to change.
- Notice that the word *mischief* has no plural.
- Experiment with deleting words in the sentences from the passage to see which are essential to meaning and which are not.

Independent work

- Children describe and sequence events in the story as a storyboard.

Plenary

- Review and discuss the children's storyboard.

DAY 2

Big Book pp. 36–37; Pupil's Book p. 57

Shared reading

- Ask the children to read the text aloud, noting how commas help the reader. Encourage them to rehearse and improve their performance.
- Experiment with ways of writing ideas in shortened form. Use key words to make headlines, e.g. Rats overrun Hamelin; Number of rats growing.

Focused word/sentence work

- Are the verbs in this story in the first, second or third person? Experiment with changing third person to first.
- Explore the strong, expressive verbs., e.g. *scuttling*, *scampering*, *gobbled*.
- As preparation for the second independent activity on page 57 in the Pupil's Book, discuss how unfamiliar words can be predicted from context.

Independent work

- Children write headlines for different parts of the story.
- Children infer the meanings of words from context, writing down their guess at meaning and checking with a dictionary.

Plenary

- Review the children's work, allowing them to reflect upon what they have learned.

DAY 3

Pupil's Book p. 58

Shared writing, including focused word/sentence work

- Page 58 in the Pupil's Book has suggestions for writing a sequel to the Pied Piper story.
- Discuss changing the setting to your school, and changing the rats to some other creature.
- Plan the story in three paragraphs. Identify typical phrases and expressions form the story to help structure the writing, e.g. Once upon a time, and this was not very long ago ...; They ate all the corn ...; They ate the cheese ...
- Encourage the children to check and improve their writing, with particular emphasis on spelling and punctuation.

Independent work

- Children write their own Pied Piper sequel.

Plenary

- Review the writing in progress.

DAY 4

Big Book pp. 38–39; Pupil's Book p. 58

Shared reading

- Read the children the extract in the Big Book from Robert Browning's *Pied Piper*. Which part of the story does the poem tell about?
- Explore the rhymes and rhythm of the poem.
- Investigate how the words suggest the rising sound of the rats leaving Hamelin.
- Ask the children to prepare the poem for reading aloud, taking note of punctuation and meaning.

Focused word/sentence work

- Look at the use of capital letters: for the beginning of each line, the river and the Piper.
- Explore the use of commas, especially in lists.
- Encourage the children to suggest likely meanings for unfamiliar words, using context clues, e.g. *adept*.

Independent work

- The children continue writing their Pied Piper sequel.

Plenary

- Review work in progress, encouraging the children to check and improve their work.

DAY 5

Big Book pp. 38–39; Pupil's Book p. 58

Shared reading

- Ask the children to read the poem aloud, encouraging appropriate expression, tone, volume and use of voice.
- Encourage the children to improve their performance, taking note of punctuation and meaning.

Focused word/sentence work

- Explore the use of adjectives. Ask the children to classify them into colour, size and mood.
- Look at the use of opposites, e.g. *great – small, lean – brawny*.

Independent work

- Children complete their writing and explore opposites on page 58 in the Pupil's Book.

Plenary

- Choose children to read aloud their Pied Piper sequels.

Homework

- Page 19 of the Homework Book has further practice on opposites.

Unit 19 Odysseus and Polyphemus

Key Learning Objectives

TL1 To investigate the styles and voices of traditional story language

TL10 To write a sequel using same characters and setting

SL4 To extend knowledge and understanding of pluralisation

SL5 To use the terms "singular" and "plural" appropriately

WL9 To investigate and identify basic rules for changing the spelling of nouns when -s is added

WL13 To recognise and spell common suffixes and how these affect meaning: -ly, -ful, -less, -ness

WL14 To use knowledge of suffixes to generate new words from root words

Range:	Greek myths
Texts:	From *The One-eyed Giant and Other Monsters from the Greek Myths*, Anne Rockwell *Heracles*
Resources:	Big Book 3B pp. 40–43 Pupil's Book 3 pp. 59–61 Homework Book 3 p. 20: Suffixes: -er, -est

DAY 1

Big Book pp. 40–41; Pupil's Book p. 60

Shared reading

- Explain to the children that this is a Greek myth in which people often meet gods, goddesses and fantastic creatures. The hero of this tale is Odysseus, who is sailing back home from Troy. The Cyclopes (/saɪˈkləʊpiːz/; plural of Cyclops) are a race of one-eyed giants. Ask the children to describe the behaviour and characteristics of Polyphemus, using the story text.

- Discuss why Polyphemus and Odysseus behaved the way they did. How would the children have reacted to the hero in the story? Ask them to justify their views.

Focused word/sentence work

- Is this a first or third person account? How can the children tell? Experiment with changing paragraph three into a first person account.

- Identify words with common suffixes, e.g. comfort*able*, furi*ous* and enorm*ous*, loud*ly*, clever*ness*. Discuss how these affect the meaning of the root word.

Independent work

- Children answer questions about the story.

Plenary

- Review the children's independent text work, showing them how to find answers from the text.

DAY 2

Big Book pp. 40–41; Pupil's Book p. 60

Shared reading

- Investigate the style and voice of the story. Note that the first paragraph is really an introduction to the Cyclopes, and Polyphemus in particular. The tale begins properly at paragraph two.

- Ask the children to identify the theme of the story: weak over strong.

- Ask the children to retell the story in their own words.

Focused word/sentence work

- Investigate the pluralisation of nouns in the story: those which simply add -s, e.g. *giants*, *laws*, *goats*; *belly*, which changes the -y to -*ies*; and *sheep*, which is an exceptional noun as it does not change when pluralised.

- Investigate the collective nouns in the story, i.e. *crew*, *flock*. Collective nouns, as collections of people, animals or things, already stand for more than one but may be further pluralised, e.g. *crews*, *flocks*. How many other examples of collective nouns from their experience or reading do the children know?

- Investigate the suffixes -*ful*, -*ness*, -*less* and -*ly*. Make a list of examples with the children's help. Discuss how these influence word meaning.

Independent work

- Children answer questions about the passage, and explore the suffixes -*ness* and -*ful*.

- The second activity on page 60 focuses on plurals: changing -*y* to -*ies*, words which do not change to make their plural, and collective nouns. Discuss the words which need to be changed when pluralising the sentences.

Plenary

- Review the work on suffixes.

DAY 3

Big Book pp. 40–41; Pupil's Book p. 61

Shared writing

- Discuss what might happen if Odysseus were forced by a storm to return to Polyphemus' island. How would the Cyclops react? How might he try to get his revenge? How would the Greeks escape?

- Plan your story in three paragraphs, using the ideas and suggestions on page 61 in the Pupil's Book.

- Collect suitable words and phrases from the original story to help structure the writing.

Focused word/sentence work

- Experiment with deleting words in selected sentences from the text to see which are essential to meaning and which are not.

- Identify words with common prefixes, e.g. *re*turn, *un*lucky, *im*possible. Discuss how these prefixes influence the meaning of the root word.

Independent work

- Children begin writing their own sequel to the story of Odysseus and Polyphemus.

Plenary

- Review the writing in progress, offering help and encouragement. Stress the need to check and revise first drafts.

DAY 4

Big Book pp. 42–43; Pupil's Book p. 61

Shared reading

- Heracles is more commonly given his Roman name, Hercules. The twelve labours were ordered by the Greek king Eurystheus, who thought the tasks were impossible and that Heracles would die.
- What was especially difficult about the first two labours? Ask the children to explain how Heracles was able to kill the two creatures.

Focused word/sentence work

- Encourage the children to use awareness of grammar and context clues to infer the meaning of unknown words.

Independent work

- Children continue or complete their sequel to the story of Odysseus and Polyphemus.

Plenary

- Read the children's sequels to the Polyphemus story.

DAY 5

Big Book pp. 42–43; Pupil's Book p. 61

Shared reading

- Ask the children to retell in their own words how Heracles defeated the Nemean Lion and the Hydra.
- Read together some of the children's sequels to the Polyphemus story.

Focused word/sentence work

- Ask the children to identify the adjectives in the text. To which nouns do they refer?
- Experiment with substituting adjectives. Which retain and which change meaning?
- Experiment with deleting adjectives. What effect does this have on meaning?

Independent work

- Children explore collective nouns on page 61 in the Pupil's Book.

Plenary

- Make a list of collective nouns suggested by the children. List them again in alphabetical order.

Consolidation and extension

- Make an illustrated class book of collective nouns, classified into people, animals and things.

Homework

- Page 20 in the Homework Book focuses on the suffixes *-er* and *-est*.

Unit 20 The Spell-Hound

Key Learning Objectives

TL1	To investigate the styles and voices of traditional story language
TL2	To identify typical story themes
TL6	To plan main points as a structure for story writing
TL8	To write portraits of characters, using story text to describe behaviour and characteristics
TL9	To write a story plan for own traditional tale
TL10	To write alternative sequels to traditional stories using same characters and settings
SL9	To experiment with deleting words in sentences to see which are essential to meaning and which are not
SL10	To understand the differences between verbs in the 1st, 2nd and 3rd person
SL11	To understand the need for grammatical agreement in speech and writing

Range:	Modern story in the style of a Viking legend
Text:	From *The Saga of Erik the Viking*, Terry Jones
Resources:	Big Book 3B pp. 44–48 Pupil's Book 3 pp. 62–64 Homework Book 3 p. 21: Key words Copymaster 20: Revision – assessment master for term 2

Preparation
- Make thesauruses available for day 2, preferably *Collins Junior Thesaurus*.

DAY 1
Big Book pp. 44–45; Pupil's Book p. 63

Shared reading
- Read the first extract from *The Saga of Erik the Viking*. Discuss the incident described.
- How can we tell the dog is supernatural? Are the sailors in real danger? Ask the children to justify their answers.
- What examples of typical traditional story language are there in the passage?
- Ask the children to improvise the scene on the Viking ship when the spell-hound is first seen, continuing it after the point where the extract ends.

Focused word/sentence work
- Investigate the specialist words connected with boats, i.e. *helm*, *tiller*. What clues are there to meaning?
- Experiment with substituting words for those in the passage. Discuss the effect on meaning, e.g. They saw a *great* black dog. Use a thesaurus to find alternative words for *great*.

Independent work
- Children answer questions about the text.

Plenary
- Monitor and assess some of the children's independent work.

DAY 2
Big Book pp. 44–45; Pupil's Book p. 63

Shared reading
- Erik is the main character in the book, but who is the most important in this extract? Ask the children to explain why.
- Investigate the style and voice of the extract.

Focused word/sentence work
- Give out a set of thesauruses. Show the children how to use the index to look up the word *glow* (page 195 in *Collins Junior Thesaurus*).
- Discuss the different shades of meaning for the synonyms listed. If the children are not sure of the precise definitions, let them use a dictionary to find out. This will have the advantage of emphasising the different functions of the two books.
- Select the most suitable words to replace *glowing* in the sentence about the spell-hound's eyes. Which work best? Why? Which are unsuitable? Why? Use the same list to discuss substituting words for *burned* in different contexts.

Independent work
- Children use thesauruses to explore synonyms on page 63 in the Pupil's Book.

Plenary
- Make a list of the synonyms the children have found for the emphasised words on page 63. Discuss their shades of meaning.

DAY 3
Big Book pp. 44–45; Pupil's Book p. 64

Shared writing
- Page 64 in the Pupil's Book has ideas for two writing activities: writing a letter to a friend describing the spell-hound and saying what happens on the voyage, and designing a poster to warn others of the spell-hound.
- Read the extract again. Ask the children to imagine they are on the ship and to describe what has already happened (giving a first person account). Point out the differences between the third person account of the text and the children's eye-witnesss account. Discuss with the children how the story might develop.
- Remind the children how to set out a letter. (See Copymaster 13.) Ask the children which person they will be writing in.
- Plan the letter together, using the notes you made earlier.

Focused word/sentence work

- Ask the class to pick out the key words, phrases and sentences which describe the spell-hound. Make a list of them to help with the writing.

Independent work

- Children begin their writing.

Plenary

- Review the writing in progress.

DAY 4

Big Book pp. 46–48; Pupil's Book p. 64

Shared reading

- Read the continuation of *The Saga of Erik the Viking* in the Big Book.
- Is this how the children expected the story to continue? How is it different from their own ideas?
- What is the theme of this story? (Trials)

Focused word/sentence work

- Remind the children how dialogue is set out in stories: speech marks, new paragraph for a different speaker, capital letters for the first word of the speech, etc.
- Experiment with deleting adjectives. How does this affect the meaning? Encourage the children to suggest substitutions.

Independent work

- Children continue or complete their writing.

Plenary

- Select children to read aloud their letters about the spell-hound.

DAY 5

Big Book pp. 46–48; Pupil's Book p. 64

Shared reading

- Ask the children to read the text aloud, using the punctuation to help them.
- Discuss ways of describing and sequencing the key incidents.

Focused word/sentence work

- Experiment with deleting words to see which are essential to meaning and which are not. Identify the key words.
- Demonstrate how the key words may be used in making notes. Explain how commas and dashes may be used to make the notes clear.

Independent work

- Children work on grammatical agreement.

Plenary

- Review the children's notes.
- Allow time for the children to reflect on what they have learned during the term.

Homework

- Page 21 in the Homework Book gives practice in identifying key words, and using them to write notes.

ASSESSMENT

Copymaster 20 is an assessment master of key word and sentence objectives for term 2, testing singular and plural, suffixes, the apostrophe in short forms and sentence construction and punctuation. Indirectly, it will also test vocabulary, general spelling and handwriting. The completed sheet will be useful as a record of progress, together with examples of the pupil's text work.

HALF-TERMLY PLANNER

Year 3 • Term 3 • Weeks 1–5

TERM 3

SCHOOL _____ CLASS _____ TEACHER _____

		Phonetics, spelling and vocabulary	Grammar and punctuation	Comprehension and composition	Texts
Continuous work Weeks 1–5		WL 1, 2, 3, 4, 5, 6, 7, 12, 17, 18, 19	SL 1		**Range** **Fiction and poetry**: Adventure and mystery stories; stories by the same author; humorous poetry, poetry that plays with language **Non-fiction**: Alphabetic texts, directories, indexes
Blocked work Week	Unit				**Titles**
1	21	WL 14, 15		TL 17, 24	From *Let's Look at Big Cats*, Rhoda Nottridge; *A Telephone Directory*; *Yellow Pages*
2	22	WL 9, 13		TL 6, 7, 15	*Rules*, Karla Kuskin; *Whipper-snapper*, Willard R. Espy; *Recipe for a Hippopotamus Sandwich*, Shel Silverstein; *Teacher said ...*, Judith Nicholls; *On the Ning Nang Nong*, Spike Milligan
3	23		SL 2, 3, 7	TL 1, 2, 3, 4, 5, 8, 9, 10, 11, 12, 14	From *Danny, the Champion of the World*, Roald Dahl; From *George's Marvellous Medicine*, Roald Dahl
4	24		SL 4, 5, 6, 7	TL 1, 2, 3, 4, 5, 8, 9, 13, 14	From *Boy*, Roald Dahl
5	25	WL 13, 14, 15	SL 2, 7	TL 1, 2, 3, 4, 5, 12	From *Jazeera in the Sun*, Lisa Bruce; From *Skull Island*, Lesley Sims

TERM 3

HALF-TERMLY PLANNER

Year 3 • Term 3 • Weeks 6–10

SCHOOL _____ CLASS _____ TEACHER _____

	Phonetics, spelling and vocabulary	Grammar and punctuation	Comprehension and composition	Texts
Continuous work Weeks 6–10	WL 1, 2, 3, 4, 5, 6, 7, 12, 17, 18, 19	SL 1		**Range** **Fiction and poetry**: Adventure and mystery stories; stories by the same author; humorous poetry, poetry that plays with language, word puzzles, puns, riddles **Non-fiction**: Letters written for a range of purposes

Blocked work Week / Unit					**Titles**
6	26			TL 17, 18, 19, 21, 24, 25, 26	*The Library*; *Food*
7	27	WL 11, 14	SL 5	TL 1, 2, 3, 4, 5, 10, 12	From *Jacqueline Hyde*, Robert Swindells
8	28		SL 6, 7	TL 1, 2, 3, 4, 5, 8, 9, 10, 11, 22	From *A Sudden Glow of Gold*, Anne Fine; From *Step by Wicked Step*, Anne Fine
9	29	WL 9, 10, 14		TL 6, 7, 15	*Strange but True*, Anon; *Wild Flowers*, Peter Newell; *Riddle*, Judith Nicholls; *UR 2 GOOD*, Michael Rosen
10	30	WL 16		TL 16, 20, 23	

Focus on Literacy Teacher's Resource Book 3 © Barry and Anita Scholes, HarperCollins*Publishers* Ltd 1999

Unit 21 Alphabetic Lists

Key Learning Objectives

TL17 To "scan" indexes, directories, etc., to locate information quickly and accurately

TL24 To make alphabetically ordered texts

WL14 To explore homonyms which have the same spelling but multiple meanings

WL15 To understand that some dictionaries provide further information about words, e.g. origins, multiple meanings, and that this can provide a guide to spelling

Range:	Alphabetic lists: index, directories
Texts:	Index from *Let's Look at Big Cats*, Rhoda Nottridge
	A Telephone Directory
	Yellow Pages
Resources:	Big Book 3C pp. 4–7
	Pupil's Book 3 pp. 65–67
	Homework Book 3 p. 22: Using a dictionary

Preparation

- For day 5 the children will need a selection of information books on wild animals, specifically on frogs, crocodiles and elephants. Check first that each book has an index.
- Make dictionaries available for day 2, preferably *Collins Primary Dictionary* or *Collins Independent Dictionary*. *Collins School Dictionary* will be useful for the information it provides on word origins. A dictionary will also be required for the activities on page 22 in the Homework Book.

DAY 1

Big Book p. 4; Pupil's Book p. 66

Shared reading

- Revise alphabetical order.
- For what kind of book is this an index? Examine the layout of the index. How is it organised? What do the numbers mean? Why are some numbers linked, e.g. *16–17*?
- Practise scanning the index to find the relevant page numbers for different subjects. Recommend that, when using an index in an information book, the children write down the subject and page numbers to save going back to the index a second or third time. This is especially important when looking up several subjects. You may wish to use a selection of information books to practise this further.

Focused word/sentence work

- Note that all the words in the index are nouns and, with two exceptions, plural. Why is that? Can the remaining nouns be made plural, e.g. *hunting*, *roaring*? (These words are *gerunds*, nouns formed from verbs, and are examples of exceptions to the rule that pluralisation is a test for nouns.)

Independent work

- Children do the index activities and alphabetical order activities on page 66 in the Pupil's Book.

Plenary

- Review the children's work.

DAY 2

Big Book p. 5; Pupil's Book p. 66

Shared reading

- Look at the layout of the (simplified) telephone directory in the Big Book. What do the abbreviations in the addresses stand for? Why are they used? Practise scanning for addresses and telephone numbers. You may wish to use a local telephone directory for further practice.

Focused word/sentence work

- Make dictionaries available. Investigate homonyms which have the same spelling, but multiple meanings, e.g. *form, mark, letter, light*. Explain how the meanings can be distinguished in context. Ask the children to suggest sentences to show the differences in meaning.
- Investigate dictionaries which explain the origins of words, e.g. *Collins School Dictionary*.

Independent work

- The children will need a dictionary for the work on page 66 in the Pupil's Book.

Plenary

- Revise the purpose and organisation of the alphabetically ordered texts examined during the lesson.
- Ask the children to make a list of other homonyms, e.g. *jet, cup, note*. Encourage them to make their own definitions for each meaning.

DAY 3

Big Book pp. 4–7; Pupil's Book p. 67

Shared writing and focused word/sentence work

- Page 67 in the Pupil's Book has a number of ideas for creating alphabetically ordered texts. Investigate examples of such texts in this unit, or in books you have collected for the purpose, e.g. information books, telephone directories.
- Select one of the ideas and plan it as a shared writing activity. Discuss how to collect, organise and present the information.
- The animal dictionary and the information book are ideal activities for children working together, but at the same time individually responsible for specific aspects. If loose-leaf books are used, new pages may be added as available. Note that the information book activity will take many sessions, and will need to be continued outside the literacy hour.

Independent work

- Children work independently on one of the alphabetically ordered texts.

Plenary

- Review the work in progress, offering help and encouragement.

DAY 4
Big Book pp. 5–7; Pupil's Book p. 67

Shared reading

- Discuss the differences between Yellow Pages and an ordinary telephone directory. Which is easier to use when looking for a particular service? Why?
- Practise finding appropriate telephone numbers for a range of services. Ask the children to make up their own questions about the text for others to answer.
- Practise scanning for addresses. Note that these are not listed alphabetically.

Focused word/sentence work

- Revise alphabetical order by playing this word game. Begin "I went to the market and bought apples." The next player repeats this and adds something beginning with *b*, e.g. "I went to the market and bought apples and biscuits." The game continues through the alphabet. Anyone who cannot remember the list, or who fails to supply an appropriate word, is out.

Independent work

- Children continue or complete their work on alphabetically organised texts.

Plenary

- Discuss some of the completed alphabetically ordered texts made by the children.
- Offer further help and encouragement to those who are still writing their texts.

DAY 5
Big Book pp. 4–7; Pupil's Book p. 67

Shared reading

- Display some of the children's completed texts. Compare them with similar texts in the Big Book or the books you have collected.
- Investigate ways of storing the children's information on computer. Compare the two kinds of text. Make a list of their respective advantages and disadvantages.

Focused word/sentence work

- Practise finding words quickly in the dictionary.

Independent work

- Make available books on frogs, crocodiles and elephants. The children are asked to scan each index for page numbers and to find the differences between an Indian and an African elephant. You might also ask them to find the differences between frogs and toads, or crocodiles and alligators.

Plenary

- Review the week's work, discussing key issues.

Homework

- Page 22 in the Homework Book gives more practice in using a dictionary.

Unit 22 — Word Play

Key Learning Objectives

- **TL6** — To compare forms or types of humour
- **TL7** — To select, prepare, read aloud and recite by heart poetry that plays with language or entertains; to recognise rhyme, alliteration and other patterns of sound that create effects
- **TL15** — To write poetry that uses sound to create effects
- **WL9** — To recognise and spell the prefixes *mis-*, *non-*, *co-* and *anti-*
- **WL13** — To collect synonyms which will be useful in writing dialogue, exploring the effects on meaning

Range:	Humorous poetry; poetry that plays with language
Texts:	*Whipper-snapper*, Willard R. Espy; *Rules*, Karla Kuski; *Teacher said ...*, Judith Nicholls; *Recipe for a Hippopotamus Sandwich*, Shel Silverstein; *On the Ning Nang Nong*, Spike Milligan
Resources:	Big Book 3C pp. 8–11 Pupil's Book 3 pp. 68–71 Homework Book 3 p. 23: Prefixes and suffixes

Preparation
- A set of thesauruses will be useful on days 2 and 3, preferably *Collins Junior Thesaurus*.

DAY 1
Big Book pp. 8–10; Pupil's Book p. 69

Shared reading
- Read the poems together. Which did the children enjoy the most? Why? Let the children read their favourites aloud.
- Discuss which categories the poems fall into: word play, joke poems, absurdities or nonsense. Do some poems fit more than one category?

Focused word/sentence work
- The poem *Whipper-snapper* is basically a list poem of double words. How many further examples of double words can the children think of?
- Investigate examples of alliteration in the poems, e.g. *grunt, grumble; shilly-shally, hippety-hoppety*.
- Ask the children to invent alliterative phrases.
- Explain what onomatopoeia is and ask the children to suggest words which sound like their meaning, e.g. *splash, rat-tat-tat, cuckoo*.

Independent work
- Children answer questions about the poems.

Plenary
- Review the children's independent work.

DAY 2
Big Book pp. 8–10; Pupil's Book p. 69

Shared reading
- Read the poem *Rules* again. Encourage the children to suggest further absurd rules.
- Did the children enjoy *Recipe for a Hippopotamus Sandwich*? Ask them to explain why. Can they think of a recipe for an equally absurd sandwich?
- Which poems rhyme? Which do not?
- Ask the children to read the poems aloud.

Focused word/sentence work
- The poem *Teacher said ...* offers an excellent opportunity to investigate common ways of introducing and concluding dialogue.
- Ask the children to put each dialogue word into a sentence to explore its meaning. Experiment with substituting other dialogue words in the children's sentences. What effect do the substitutions have on meaning?
- Ask the children to classify the words in the poem, e.g. loud and soft ways of speaking.

Independent work
- Page 69 in the Pupil's Book investigates synonyms and rhymes.

Plenary
- Review the children's independent work on synonyms.

DAY 3
Big Book pp. 8–10; Pupil's Book p. 70

Shared writing and focused word/sentence work
- Page 70 in the Pupil's Book has ideas for using the poems in this unit as models for the children's own. The first four suggestions are for the poems already studied, while the fifth activity is best reserved until day 4, after *On the Ning Nang Nong* has been read.
- Select one of the poems, or ask the children to choose. Read it through and discuss its pattern. Encourage the children to substitute their own ideas for those of the poem. A thesaurus will be useful if you are writing a *Teacher said ...* poem.
- Work together to write a class poem.

Independent work
- Children write their own poem using one of the poems as a model.

Plenary
- Ask those children who have finished their poems to read them aloud. Offer help and encouragement.

DAY 4

Big Book p. 11; Pupil's Book pp. 70–71

Shared reading/writing, including focused word/sentence work

- Read *On the Ning Nang Nong*. Then ask the children to read the poem aloud. Discuss different ways of doing this, perhaps with a small group as narrator and other small groups of children to read only the amusing sound words. This may be developed for performance to other classes.
- Pick out the sound words. Make a list of the words which rhyme.
- Discuss ways of using this poem as a model, as outlined on page 69 in the Pupil's Book.
- Discuss aspects such as alliteration, onomatopoeia, rhythm and synonyms.

Independent work

- Children write their own version of *On the Ning Nang Nong*, or continue with their poems from day 3.

Plenary

- Select children to read aloud their completed poems.

DAY 5

Big Book pp. 8–11; Pupil's Book p. 71

Shared reading

- Ask the children to select their favourite poems from this unit for reading aloud.
- Encourage the children to read aloud their own completed poems, making sure that at least one example of each model is read.
- Discuss the children's own poems in an atmosphere of constructive criticism.

Focused word/sentence work

- Investigate words with the prefixes *mis-*, *ex-*, *non-*, *co-* and *anti-*.

Independent work

- Children explore the prefixes *mis-*, *non-*, *co-* and *anti-* on page 71 in the Pupil's Book.

Plenary

- Review the week's work.

Consolidation and extension

- Make a big book of the children's poems.

Homework

- Page 23 in the Homework Book focuses on prefixes and suffixes.

Unit 23   Hiding in the Dark

Key Learning Objectives

TL1	To re-tell main points of story in sequence; to compare different stories; to evaluate stories and justify preference
TL2	To refer to significant aspects of the text, and to know language is used to create these
TL3	To distinguish between 1st and 3rd person accounts
TL4	To consider credibility of events
TL5	To discuss characters' feelings, behaviour and relationships; referring to the text and making judgements
TL8	To compare works by the same author
TL9	To be aware of authors and to discuss preferences and reasons for these
TL10	To plot a sequence of episodes modelled on a known story, as a plan for writing
TL11	To write openings to stories or chapters linked to or arising from reading; to focus on language to create effects
TL12	To write a first person account
TL14	To write book reviews for a specified audience, based on evaluations of plot, characters, language
SL2	To identify pronouns and understand their functions in sentences
SL3	To ensure grammatical agreement in speech and writing of pronouns and verbs
SL7	To become aware of the use of commas in marking grammatical boundaries within sentences

Range:	Adventure stories; stories by the same author
Texts:	From *Danny, the Champion of the World*, Roald Dahl From *George's Marvellous Medicine*, Roald Dahl
Resources:	Big Book 3C pp. 12–15 Pupil's Book 3 pp. 72–74 Homework Book 3 p. 24: Pronouns Copymaster 21: Book review: plot and theme Copymaster 22: Book review: incident and character

DAY 1

Big Book pp. 12–13; Pupil's Book p. 73

Shared reading

- Read the extract from *Danny, the Champion of the World* and discuss how a small boy came to be driving a car at half past two in the morning. Is this situation credible? Ask the children to suggest how Danny might have learned how to drive. Those who have read the book will know that Danny's dad repaired cars and that he allowed Danny to move them in and out of the workshop. (This was off the road and therefore legal.)
- Is this a first or third person account? How can we tell?
- Ask the children to retell the events in the extract as a third person account.

Focused word/sentence work

- Look for examples of compound words, e.g. *policeman, headlamps, sideways*. Note that some compound words are hyphenated, e.g. *filling-station*.
- Investigate the use of commas in the passage, e.g. to mark grammatical boundaries within sentences.
- Investigate how words and phrases can signal time sequences: Then all at once …; The first thing I did …; now …

Independent work

- Page 73 in the Pupil's Book has comprehension questions on the extract.

Plenary

- Review the children's independent work, reminding them how to find facts and clues in the text.

DAY 2

Big Book pp. 12–13; Pupil's Book p. 73

Shared reading

- Discuss why Danny behaved as he did, and how he felt. Was his behaviour reasonable? What would the children have done in the same circumstances?

Focused word/sentence work

- Pick out the adjectives in the passage. Which describe size? (E.g. tiny, thick, narrow.)
- Explain to the children what a pronoun is and how and why they are used.
- Ask the children to pick out the pronouns from the passage, e.g. *I, he, me, you, it*. Are these singular or plural?
- Classify the pronouns into first, second and third person.

Independent work

- Page 73 in the Pupil's Book has work on pronouns.

Plenary

- Review the children's work on pronouns.

DAY 3

Big Book pp. 12–13; Pupil's Book p. 74

Shared reading/writing, including focused word/sentence work

- Ask the children to pick out words and phrases which make the passage exciting.
- Ask them to predict what will happen next.
- Demonstrate how to plan a story using one of the methods described on page 74 in the Pupil's Book.
- Brainstorm a list of suitable words to build up atmosphere in your story.
- Encourage the children to consider the consequences of the main character's actions in the story.

Independent work

- Children plan their own story to extend the event in the extract, writing in the first person with themselves as the central character.

Plenary

- Review the children's story planning, offering help and encouragement.

DAY 4

Big Book pp. 14–15; Pupil's Book p. 74

Shared reading

- Read the extract from *George's Marvellous Medicine* on pages 14–15 of the Big Book. Is this story more, or less, credible than that of Danny? What makes the children think so?
- In which person is this extract written?
- In what other ways is this story different from the Danny extract?

Focused word/sentence work

- Ask the children to pick out the words and phrases which build up atmosphere. Classify them into adjectives, verbs and nouns. Classify the adjectives further into sight, smell and feeling.
- Ask the children to identify the pronouns.

Independent work

- Children use their story plans to begin or continue their writing.

Plenary

- Review the children's writing, offering help and encouragement.

DAY 5

Big Book pp. 14–15; Pupil's Book p. 74

Shared reading

- What do the children think of George's behaviour? Is he sensible to make such a mixture? Ask the children to justify their answers.
- What does the fact that he is going to try this mixture on his grandmother tell us about George's relationship with her?
- Encourage the children to read the extract aloud, using the punctuation to help them.
- Ask the children which other Roald Dahl books they have read. Which is their favourite? Why?

Focused word/sentence work

- Investigate how words and phrases can signal time sequences: *soon, whenever, at one point, suddenly*.
- Revise pronouns in preparation for the independent work.

Independent work

- Children complete their stories.
- Page 74 in the Pupil's Book focuses on singular and plural pronouns, and helps the children understand the need for grammatical agreement between pronoun and verb.

Plenary

- Re-emphasise teaching points on pronouns.

Consolidation and extension

- Ask some children to prepare and read aloud their extensions to the Danny story.
- Revise pronouns by giving the children sentences with singular pronouns to change into plural and vice versa. Discuss the need for grammatical agreement of pronoun and verb.
- Copymaster 21 is a book review focusing on retelling the main events of a book in sequence and identifying its theme. Specify an audience and purpose for the review, e.g. to encourage other children in the class to read the book.
- Copymaster 22 is an alternative book review focusing on a significant incident, the words used to create effect, and the feelings and behaviour of the main character. Suggest a purpose and audience for the review.

Homework

- Page 24 in the Homework Book consolidates the work on pronouns.

Unit 24 — The Great Mouse Plot

Key Learning Objectives

TL1	To re-tell main points of story in sequence; to compare different stories; to evaluate stories and justify preference
TL2	To refer to significant aspects of the text, and to know language is used to create these
TL3	To distinguish between 1st and 3rd person accounts
TL4	To consider credibility of events
TL5	To discuss characters' feelings, behaviour and relationships; referring to the text and making judgements
TL8	To compare works by the same author
TL9	To be aware of authors and to discuss preferences and reasons for these
TL13	To write more extended stories based on a plan of incidents and set out in simple chapters with titles and author details; to use paragraphs to organise the narrative
TL14	To write book reviews for a specified audience, based on evaluations of plot, characters, language
SL4	To use speech marks and other dialogue punctuation appropriately in writing and to use the conventions which mark boundaries between spoken words and the rest of the sentence
SL5	To understand how sentences can be joined in more complex ways, using a widening range of conjunctions: *so, while, since, when*
SL6	To investigate through reading and writing how words and phrases can signal time sequences.
SL7	To become aware of the use of commas in marking grammatical boundaries within sentences

Range:	Real life adventure retold as a story
Texts:	From *Boy*, Roald Dahl
Resources:	Big Book 3C pp. 16–19
	Pupil's Book 3 pp. 75–77
	Homework Book 3 p. 25: Using speech marks and other punctuation
	Copymaster 23: Finding out about an author: Roald Dahl
	Copymaster 24: Comparing books by the same author

Preparation

- The weekly plan of work is slightly different in this unit because the writing of an extended story will begin on day 3. As this will need more time in shared planning and writing it is better to allocate day 4 for shared writing too, with only day 5 for shared reading of the second text.
- The extended writing will require further time outside the literacy hour.

DAY 1

Big Book pp. 16–17; Pupil's Book p. 76

Shared reading

- Explain to the children that this account by Roald Dahl is a real-life incident. How does it compare with incidents in the author's fiction books? Is it more credible, or less? Is it as exciting? Ask the children to justify their answers.
- Is this a first or a third person account? How can the class tell?
- Pick out the words and phrases which make the incident exciting.
- What does the class think of the behaviour of the boys, and the part Roald Dahl plays in particular? Was it brave, foolish or reasonable? How does the incident make the writer feel? How does it change the relationship between him and the other boys?

Focused word/sentence work

- Explore words and phrases which can signal time sequences: *now, then, when, as soon as.*
- Explore the use of the apostrophe in contractions. Explain why Roald Dahl uses the apostrophe for Mrs Pratchett's words: "I don't want all the lot of you troopin' in 'ere if only one of you is buyin'."

Independent work

- Children answer questions on the text.

Plenary

- Review the children's independent work, reminding them how to find facts and clues in the text.

DAY 2

Big Book pp. 16–17; Pupil's Book p. 76

Shared reading

- Discuss the probable consequences of The Great Mouse Plot.
- Ask the children to talk about their favourite Roald Dahl books, giving preferences and reasons.
- Discuss the similarities and differences between two Roald Dahl books the children know well.
- Copymaster 23 helps children become more aware of authors by encouraging them to find out more about Roald Dahl from book covers and other sources.
- Copymaster 24 helps children who have read two books by the same author to compare and contrast them, and to give preferences and reasons.

Focused word/sentence work

- Investigate how sentences can be joined in more complex ways through using a widening range of conjunctions: *so, while, when.*
- Examine the use of commas to mark grammatical boundaries within sentences.

- Investigate the punctuation of the dialogue: speech marks and the commas, question marks or exclamation marks which mark the boundaries between spoken words and the rest of the sentence.
- Find the alternative words for *said* which Roald Dahl uses: *screamed, shouted, cried.*

Independent work
- Children explore the use of speech marks and other associated punctuation, and use the conjunctions *when, while* and *since* to join the sentences on page 76 in the Pupil's Book.

Plenary
- Review the children's work on speech marks and conjunctions, re-emphasising teaching points and clarifying misconceptions.

DAY 3
Big Book pp. 16–17; Pupil's Book p. 77

Shared writing, including focused word/sentence work
- Page 77 in the Pupil's Book has suggestions for planning an extended story written by a team of writers, one chapter each.
- Discuss a plot for the story, perhaps drawing inspiration from The Great Mouse Plot by inventing a school children's prank which goes wrong, with unexpected or disastrous consequences.
- The story will need detailed planning, chapter by chapter, so that each writer knows what happens before and after his or her own chapter. The story plan should be displayed prominently for reference, together with a list of authors.
- Each chapter should then be planned in three paragraphs. It may be written by a single child or in pairs, perhaps teaming children of different abilities.
- Encourage revision of the writing.
- Select a small editorial team to check that the story flows consistently between chapters without sudden changes in plot, character or setting.
- Collate the chapters and publish the story as a book, with font cover illustrations, back cover blurb, a list of chapter titles and authors, illustrations, etc.
- This activity will take a number of sessions and may be continued outside the literacy hour, perhaps as homework.

Independent work
- Children work on ideas for the extended story.

Plenary
- Review the children's planning.

DAY 4
Big Book pp. 16–17; Pupil's Book p. 77

Shared writing, including focused word/sentence work
- Use day 4 to continue the shared planning of the extended story.

Independent work
- Children plan and write their individual chapters for the extended story.

Plenary
- Review the children's planning and writing, offering help and encouragement.

DAY 5
Big Book pp. 18–19; Pupil's Book p. 77

Shared reading
- Read the further extract from *Boy*. What appears to have happened when Mrs Pratchett found the mouse? Ask the children to use evidence from the text.
- Explore how Roald Dahl builds suspense by gradually revealing the scene in the sweet shop: the "closed" sign, the missing jar on the shelf, the jar smashed on the floor, and finally the mouse lying in the wreckage.
- What do the children think will happen next?
- Encourage the children to make a top five (or more) list of their favourite Roald Dahl books, with reasons why they enjoyed them. Which books are similar? Compare and contrast settings, characters, plots and themes. Which two of his books feature the same characters?

Focused word/sentence work
- Pick out the words and phrases which create atmosphere.
- Examine the use of speech marks and associated punctuation for dialogue.

Independent work
- Children continue writing.

Plenary
- Reflect upon and discuss the week's sentence work: speech marks and conjunctions.
- Monitor progress on the extended writing.

Consolidation and extension
- Copymaster 23 helps children become more aware of authors by encouraging them to find out more about Roald Dahl from book covers and other sources.
- Copymaster 24 helps children who have read two books by the same author to compare and contrast them, and to give preferences and reasons.

Homework
- Page 25 in the Homework Book consolidates using speech marks and other dialogue punctuation.

Unit 25 A Snake in the Garden

Key Learning Objectives

TL1	To re-tell main points of story in sequence; to compare different stories; to evaluate stories and justify preference
TL2	To refer to significant aspects of the text, and to know language is used to create these
TL3	To distinguish between 1st and 3rd person accounts
TL4	To consider credibility of events
TL5	To discuss characters' feelings, behaviour and relationships; referring to the text and making judgements
TL12	To write a first person account: a character's own account of incident in a story
SL2	To identify pronouns and understand their functions in sentences
SL7	To become aware of the use of commas in marking grammatical boundaries within sentences
WL13	To collect synonyms which will be useful in writing dialogue
WL14	To explore homonyms which have the same spelling but multiple meanings
WL15	To understand that some dictionaries provide further information about words: multiple meanings

Range:	Adventure and mystery stories
Texts:	From *Jazeera in the Sun*, Lisa Bruce From *Skull Island*, Lesley Sims
Resources:	Big Book 3C pp. 20–23 Pupil's Book 3 pp. 78–80 Homework Book 3 p. 26: Homonyms

Preparation
- Make a dictionary available for day 5, preferably *Collins Primary Dictionary* or *Collins Independent Dictionary*.

DAY 1
Big Book pp. 20–21; Pupil's Book p. 79

Shared reading
- Read the extract to the children and ask them to retell it in their own words.
- Is this story credible? Why?
- Is this a first or third person account? Ask the children to justify their answer.
- Who is the main character? How do the children know? We see the events from Jazeera's point of view. We are told what she is thinking and feeling. What words and phrases tell us this?
- Has any of the class felt the way Jazeera felt? What happened to make them feel that way?

Focused word/sentence work
- Collect adjectives from the extract. Classify them for colour, shape, texture, mood, etc.
- Investigate the use of commas in marking grammatical boundaries in sentences.
- Explore changing word order to keep the same meaning, e.g. *Shaken by the attack, the snake slithered out*. Note the use of the comma to mark the boundary between the two parts of the sentence.
- Why is *Frisbee* spelt with a capital letter? (It is a registered trade name.)

Independent work
- Children answer questions on the text.

Plenary
- Review the children's independent work, reminding them how to find facts and clues in the text.

DAY 2
Big Book pp. 20–21; Pupil's Book p. 79

Shared reading
- Ask the children to pick out words and phrases which make the incident exciting.
- Why did Jazeera behave the way she did? Was it brave? sensible? foolish? What do they think of Anil's behaviour? Why did he not want Jazeera to throw the Frisbee? Ask the children to justify their answers.
- How did Jazeera feel towards Anil when she backed away from the bush? How did she feel when he had driven the snake off?

Focused word/sentence work
- Identify the common pronouns in the extract. Which nouns do they stand for?
- Distinguish between personal pronouns (*I, you, he, she, it, we, they, me, him, her, us, them*) and possessive pronouns (*mine, yours, his, hers, ours, theirs*).
- Ask the children to put these pronouns in sentences of their own.

Independent work
- The cloze passage from *Jazeera in the Sun* continues the story. All the missing words are personal pronouns. Encourage the children to infer from both context and grammar, e.g. verb agreement, gender clues.
- The second activity on page 79 focuses on possessive pronouns.

Plenary
- Review the children's work on the cloze passage.
- Revise the distinction between personal and possessive pronouns. Clarify any misconceptions.

DAY 3

Big Book pp. 20–21; Pupil's Book p. 80

Shared writing, including focused word/sentence work

- Read the the extract again. Ask the class to consider what Jazeera and Anil were thinking and feeling at each point in the story.
- Ask them to imagine they are either Jazeera or Anil and to tell the story in their own words (a first person account). Use the pictures and corresponding questions on page 80 of the Pupil's Book to help the children focus on each part of the story.
- Use the ideas generated to make a plan for the story in three paragraphs.
- Discuss how to describe the setting: a garden of a house in India. What sort of climate is that?
- Write the first paragraph together, encouraging the children to choose words which will build up atmosphere and express feelings.

Independent work

- Children write a character's own account of the snake in the garden incident.

Plenary

- Review the children's writing, offering help and encouragement.

DAY 4

Big Book pp. 22–23; Pupil's Book p. 80

Shared reading

- Read the extract from *Skull Island*. Is this a first or third person account?
- Ask the children to retell the story in their own words.
- Ask the children to pick out the words and phrases which build up the suspense.

Focused word/sentence work

- Which synonyms for *said* help to make the story exciting? E.g. *yelled, gasped, panted*.
- Explore the use of commas in marking grammatical boundaries in sentences.
- Pick out the pronouns in the text. Which nouns do they stand for?

Independent work

- Children continue or complete their writing from day 3.

Plenary

- Ask some children to read their completed stories to the class. Provide feedback and encouragement.

DAY 5

Big Book pp. 22–23; Pupil's Book p. 80

Shared reading

- Was Ben wise to shout "Over here!" to their pursuers? Ask the children to give reasons for their answers.
- Which words give clues to the thoughts and feelings of the children?
- Who do the children think Zack might be?

Focused word/sentence work

- Explore substituting alternative adjectives for those in the text. How does this change meaning?
- Do the same with alternative verbs.
- Use a dictionary to explore homonyms in the text: words with the same spelling but multiple meanings, e.g. *run, dart, head, face, fast, beat*.

Independent work

- Children explore homonyms on page 80 in the Pupil's Book.

Plenary

- Re-emphasise the main teaching points for the week's work.
- Allow the children to present and discuss key issues in their work.

Homework

- Page 26 in the Homework Book consolidates the work on homonyms.

Unit 26 The Library

Key Learning Objectives

TL17 To "scan" indexes to locate information quickly and accurately

TL18 To locate books by classification in class or school libraries

TL19 To summarise orally in one sentence the content of a passage or text, and the main point it is making

TL21 To use IT to bring work to a published form

TL24 To make an alphabetically ordered text, using information derived from other information books

TL25 To revise and extend work on note-making from previous term

TL26 To summarise in writing the content of a passage or text and the main point it is making

Range:	Library classification system
Texts:	*Fiction books*
	Non-fiction books
	Food
Resources:	Big Book 3C pp. 24–29
	Pupil's Book 3 pp. 81–83
	Homework Book 3 p. 27: Fiction and non-fiction
	Copymaster 25: Finding fiction books; awareness of author
	Copymaster 26: Finding non-fiction books

Preparation

- Select in advance a variety of fiction and non-fiction books from the class or school library for the children to sort. These will be required from day 1.
- Make available a selection of books on birds, reptiles, fish and pets for days 3, 4 and 5.
- Prepare IT reference sources on the same subjects for days 3, 4 and 5.
- Note that this unit is planned for the second text in the Big Book to be read on day 2, and the writing activity beginning on day 3 to continue through the rest of the week. Further time will be required outside the literacy hour to complete the writing.

DAY 1

Big Book pp. 24–27; Pupil's Book p. 82

Shared reading

- Make available a selection of fiction and non-fiction books. Teach the difference between fiction and non-fiction books. What clues does a book give, e.g. title, cover, organisation, contents page, index? Ask the children to sort the titles on page 26 in the Big Book into fiction and non-fiction. Ask them to justify their choices.
- Teach how fiction books are classified in public libraries. Revise alphabetical order. If you have a school library with a different system, explain how it works.
- Teach how non-fiction books are classified, i.e. in topics, according to the Dewey system, etc. Use the topic webs on page 81 of the Pupil's Book to show how topics may be further divided into sub-topics. Ask the children to suggest further sub-topics to complete the webs. Ask them to match the list of sub-topics to their correct webs.

Focused word/sentence work

- Revise alphabetical order to the second letter. Ask the children to make a list of their favourite authors and then to arrange them in alphabetical order.

Independent work

- Children answer questions about library organisation.

Plenary

- Review the children's independent work.

DAY 2

Big Book pp. 28–29; Pupil's Book p. 82

Shared reading

- Look together at the Food text on page 28 in the Big Book, which is also reproduced in the Pupil's Book on page 82. What is the main idea of each paragraph? How can we tell?
- Make a list of facts which support each main idea, by picking out the key words.
- Ask the children to use the list to retell the information in complete sentences.

Focused word/sentence work

- Remind the children of the need for alphabetical order when locating fiction books.
- In what ways is a knowledge of alphabetical order useful when using information books?

Independent work

- Page 82 in the Pupil's Book gives practice in sorting fiction books, and in making notes on the Food passage.

Plenary

- Review the children's independent work.

DAY 3

Pupil's Book p. 83

Shared writing, including focused word and sentence work

- Page 83 in the Pupil's Book has ideas for the children to make their own information books on birds, reptiles, fish or pets. Make available a selection of suitable information books for the class to use as reference. IT sources will also be useful.

- Explain how the main topic of an information book is broken down into sub-topics, e.g. *pets* into *cats*, *dogs*, *fish*.
- Select one of the main topics, e.g. *birds*, and four sub-topics. Write the three headings: *Description*, *Habitat*, *Food*, and use the information in one or more books to make notes. Remind the children of the importance of key words when writing notes.
- Explain how the notes can then be used to make a short information book, with a contents page and an index. The book only requires four leaves/eight pages if a page is devoted to each of the four sub-topics. The contents, index and two covers will then complete the book. The number of pages may be extended by including illustrations or further topics according to the interests of the children.
- Remind the children of the need to use alphabetical order for the index.
- This activity will continue on days 4 and 5 and will need further time outside the literacy hour.

Independent work
- Children begin work on their information books.

Plenary
- Review the work in progress, offering help and encouragement.

DAY 4
Pupil's Book p. 83

Shared writing
- Use the selection of fiction and non-fiction books you have collected to investigate the parts of a book and how these help the reader.
- Are there any obvious differences between the covers of fiction and non-fiction books? How are the contents pages different?
- Examine and discuss the different ways non-fiction books are organised.

Focused word/sentence work
- Offer appropriate help and encouragement with relevant word and sentence issues from the children's writing.

Independent work
- Children continue writing.

Plenary
- Review the work in progress, offering help and encouragement. Use good examples of the pupils' drafts to emphasise teaching points.

DAY 5
Pupil's Book p. 83

Shared reading/writing
- Look again at the selection of fiction and non-fiction books you have collected. Do they all have an index? How useful is an index? Give practice in using an index to locate information.
- Show how to construct an index for the children's information books.
- Compare information books with IT sources. How are they different? Discuss their relative advantages and disadvantages.
- Encourage the use of IT to bring the children's work to a published form. Discuss the relevance of layout, font, etc.

Focused word/sentence work
- Emphasise the need for the children to check and correct their work.

Independent work
- Children continue writing their books. They will need further time outside the literacy hour to complete them.

Plenary
- Review the work in progress. Offer help and encouragement.

Consolidation and extension
- Copymaster 25 gives practice in finding fiction books in a library. Using this sheet and examining book covers may stimulate the children to try authors new to them.
- Discuss the fiction titles listed by the children on Copymaster 25. How many of the authors have they read? How many names are new to them? Which books caught their interest? Why?
- Copymaster 26 offers similar practice in finding non-fiction books. The children are asked to list two books. Point out that they may use book titles on sub-topics of the main topic given, e.g. *a football book* for *sport*, *butterflies* for *insects*, *castles* for *buildings*.
- Display the children's own information books. Add them to the class library.

Homework
- Page 27 in the Homework Book consolidates work on library classification into fiction and non-fiction.

Unit 27 Jacqueline Hyde

Key Learning Objectives

TL1	To re-tell main points of story in sequence; to compare different stories; to evaluate stories and justify preference
TL2	To refer to significant aspects of the text, and to know language is used to create these
TL3	To distinguish between 1st and 3rd person accounts
TL4	To consider credibility of events
TL5	To discuss characters' feelings, behaviour and relationships; referring to the text and making judgements
TL10	To plot a sequence of episodes modelled on a known story, as a plan for writing
TL12	To write a first person account
SL5	To explore how sentences can be joined in more complex ways using a widening range of conjunctions: *so, if, though*
WL11	To use the apostrophe to spell further contracted forms
WL14	To explore homonyms which have the same spelling but multiple meanings

Range:	Adventure/mystery story
Texts:	From *Jacqueline Hyde*, Robert Swindells
Resources:	Big Book 3C pp. 30–34 Pupil's Book 3 pp. 84–87 Homework Book 3 p. 28: Joining sentences

Preparation
- Make a dictionary available for day 2.

DAY 1
Big Book pp. 30–32; Pupil's Book p. 85

Shared reading
- When you have read the story, ask the children if anyone has read *Dr Jekyll and Mr Hyde* by Robert Louis Stevenson, a story with a similar theme. What was that book about? Why do they think the author chose the name Jacqueline for his main character?
- Is this a first or third person account?
- Ask the children to retell the events which led to Jacqueline Good turning into Jacqueline Hyde.
- Was it sensible of Jacqueline to open and sniff the old medicine bottle? Ask the class to describe how she felt as she sniffed it. At what point is it clear that this new energy is a force for evil? Ask the children to find words and phrases from the passage which describe these events.
- Which words and phrases in the passage build up atmosphere?

Focused word/sentence work
- Experiment with transforming selected sentences from the passage from first to third person. Discuss the changes that need to be made for grammatical agreement.
- Investigate the adjectives in the passage. Explore ways of substituting others. Use a thesaurus to explore possible synonyms.

Independent work
- Page 85 in the Pupil's Book has a cloze passage from *Jacqueline Hyde* in which all the missing words are adjectives. Please note that any words which fit the sense and the grammar are acceptable. The original words are given here for reference and/or for later discussion:
1) electric, 2) dirty, 3) broken, 4) ancient, 5) dusty, 6) mouldering, 7) small, 8) mildewed, 9) rusty, 10) cracked, 11) plastic, 12) pretty, 13) dirty.

Plenary
- Discuss the adjectives the children have suggested for the cloze passage. Compare these with those of the author (see above).

DAY 2
Big Book pp. 30–32; Pupil's Book p. 85

Shared reading
- Jacqueline says "Grandma will be pleased." What does she mean by that? How does the class think Grandma will react when Jacqueline comes down from the loft? How might Jacqueline react? How might this change their relationship?
- Why has the author put the word *hated* in italics in the sentence "*Hated* it." What does this tell us about the changed Jacqueline?
- Is this story credible? Ask the children to justify their answers.

Focused word/sentence work
- Explore the use of the apostrophe in contractions: *wasn't, couldn't*, etc.
- Investigate the use of conjunctions in the text: *so, and, but*. Discuss how sentences can be joined using *so, if, although* and *though*. Introduce the children to the work on page 87 in the Pupil's Book.
- Ask the children to pick out compound words from the text. Point out that some compound words are hyphenated, e.g. *tea-chests*.
- Ask the children to pick out homonyms from the passage and explore their different meanings, e.g. *hard, iron, right, pass, good*.

Independent work
- Children identify compound words in the text and use them in sentences of their own.
- Children explore homonyms. Make available a dictionary to help with this activity.

Plenary

- Review the children's independent work, correcting any misconceptions.

DAY 3
Big Book pp. 30–34; Pupil's Book pp. 86–87

Shared writing, including focused word and sentence work

- Pages 86–87 in the Pupil's Book invite the children to put themselves in Jacqueline's place, writing what happens now she is no longer the well-behaved girl she was, and exploring the consequences of this change in her behaviour.
- Read the first extract again. Draw attention to the fact that the story is written in the first person in a conversational tone. Note the use of expressions such as "you wouldn't believe me anyway", and the colloquial "There was this mirror."
- Ask the children to retell the story to the class as if they were Jacqueline talking to a friend.
- Read the second extract on pages 33–34 in the Big Book, which tells how Jacqueline felt as she set off down the street "looking for fun". Discuss the effect of the bottle on the way she feels, and what this might make her do.
- Make a list of ideas, organising them into three paragraphs.
- Ask the children to write their stories in a similar conversational style to the extract, as if they were talking to a friend. Encourage them to use colloquialisms and shortened forms using the apostrophe.

Independent work

- Children begin their writing.

Plenary

- Review the children's writing, offering help and encouragement. Make sure the children are describing Jacqueline's thoughts and feelings. Are they writing in Jacqueline's conversational style?

DAY 4
Big Book pp. 33–34; Pupil's Book pp. 86–87

Shared reading

- Read the second extract again. How does Jacqueline's behaviour to her grandma show that she has changed?
- Explore the language which describes Jacqueline's heightened senses. Which words and phrases are particularly effective?

Focused word/sentence work

- Discuss substituting adjectives and verbs for those in the passage, e.g. *sharp*, *glistened*, *motored*. How does this change meaning?

Independent work

- Children continue writing their story.

Plenary

- Ask some children to read aloud their completed stories, or a completed paragraph.

DAY 5
Big Book pp. 33–34; Pupil's Book p. 87

Shared reading

- We are not told how Grandma reacted when Jacqueline came down from the loft, but discuss how she might have felt. What would she think of Jacqueline's behaviour?
- Ask the children to retell the incident from Grandma's point of view in a conversational style.

Focused word/sentence work

- Look at examples of the use of the apostophe in contractions: *didn't*, the *exercise'll* be good for your rheumatism, *must've*.
- Revise the conjunctions *so*, *if* and *though* in preparation for the independent work.

Independent work

- Children work on joining sentences in more complex ways, using the conjunctions *so*, *if* and *though*.

Plenary

- Ask the children to read aloud their Jacqueline stories. Draw attention to good examples of conversational style, descriptions of feelings and sensations, etc.

Consolidation and extension

- Record the best of the children's stories on tape.

Homework

- Page 28 in the Homework Book gives further practice in using the conjunctions *so*, *if* and *although*.

Unit 28 — A Sudden Glow of Gold

Key Learning Objectives

TL1	To re-tell main points of story in sequence; to compare different stories; to evaluate stories and justify preference
TL2	To refer to significant aspects of the text, and to know language is used to create these
TL3	To distinguish between 1st and 3rd person accounts
TL4	To consider credibility of events
TL5	To discuss characters' feelings, behaviour and relationships; referring to the text and making judgements
TL8	To compare works by the same author
TL9	To be aware of authors and to discuss preferences and reasons for these
TL10	To plot a sequence of episodes modelled on a known story, as a plan for writing
TL11	To write openings to stories or chapters linked to or arising from reading; to focus on language to create effects
TL22	To experiment with recounting the same event in a different way
SL6	To investigate through reading and writing how words and phrases can signal time sequences: *first, then, after, meanwhile, from, when*
SL7	To become aware of the use of commas in marking grammatical boundaries within sentences

Range:	Adventure and mystery stories; stories by same author
Texts:	From *A Sudden Glow of Gold*, Anne Fine From *Step by Wicked Step*, Anne Fine
Resources:	Big Book 3C pp. 35–39 Pupil's Book 3 pp. 88–90 Homework Book 3 p. 29: Compound words

DAY 1

Big Book pp. 35–37; Pupil's Book p. 89

Shared reading

- Read the extract from *A Sudden Glow of Gold*. Is this a first or third person account?
- Could this story really happen? Ask the children to justify their answers.
- How is the genie in this story different from those in traditional stories? Ask the children to justify their answers, quoting words and phrases from the passage. What sort of relationship do they think Toby will have with the genie? What makes them think so?

Focused word/sentence work

- Collect compound words from the extract, e.g. *birdsong, fingernail, bedroom*. What other compound words can the children think of? E.g. *classroom, blackboard, cupboard*.

- Look at the use of speech marks and other dialogue punctuation. Notice that some sentences do not have any indication of who is speaking. Why is this?
- Investigate the use of commas in marking grammatical boundaries within sentences.

Independent work

- Children answer questions on the text.

Plenary

- Review the children's comprehension work.

DAY 2

Big Book pp. 35–37; Pupil's Book p. 89

Shared reading

- How did Toby feel when he met the genie? Which words tell us?
- How did the genie feel about Toby and his room? Which words show this?
- Which words and phrases in the passage describe the change in the atmosphere of the room when the genie appeared? Why was Toby slow to realise the change?

Focused word/sentence work

- Explore words in the passage which signal time sequences: *at first, now*. What other words can be used to indicate time sequence? E.g. *then, after, next, meanwhile, in the meantime, at the same time, soon, when, later, before*.
- Introduce the children to the cloze passage on page 89 in the Pupil's Book. This time the missing words are of many kinds: nouns, conjunctions, verbs, prepositions, etc. Encourage the children to read past the missing word, as well as up to it, when making their predictions.

Independent work

- Children complete the cloze passage on page 89 of the Pupil's Book, and explore the use of words that signal time sequence.

Plenary

- Review the children's cloze work. Any word that fits the sense of the passage and the grammar of the sentence is acceptable, but the author's words are given here for reference and discussion purposes: 1) moment, 2) genie, 3) chocolate, 4) on, 5) because, 6) from, 7) the, 8) he, 9) really, 10) flesh, 11) metal, 12) think, 13) away, 14) bedroom.

DAY 3

Big Book pp. 35–37; Pupil's Book p. 90

Shared writing, including focused word/sentence work

- Read the story of Toby and the genie again.
- Explore the use of the apostrophe in short foms.
- Revise and practise the use of words to signal time by asking the children to retell the story of Toby and the genie using these time words: *at first, then, soon, suddenly, finally*.
- Discuss what might happen if the children were to find a magic lamp.
- Look at the story planner on page 90 in the Pupil's Book. Use the questions and pictures to consider various scenarios.
- Write a plan for the story. Brainstorm words and phrases which will set the scene and create atmosphere. Refer to the extract to see ways in which this can be done.
- Encourage the children to suggest an interesting ending.
- Encourage the children to remember to use punctuation correctly in their writing.

Independent work

- Children begin their writing.

Plenary

- Review the children's writing, offering help and encouragement.

DAY 4

Big Book pp. 38–39; Pupil's Book p. 90

Shared reading

- Read the second extract in the Big Book, which is also from an Anne Fine book. What feelings do the children get from the text? Which words and phrases create this feeling?
- In stories and films old and possibly haunted houses are frequently seen during a thunderstorm. Why do the children think writers and film-makers do this? What is dramatic about a thunderstorm? How do they make people feel? Is this feeling then carried over to the setting?
- Is the story believable? Ask the children to justify their answers.
- What do the children think might happen next?

Focused word/sentence work

- Look for examples of words which signal time: *even before, as, suddenly, after*.
- Investigate the use of commas in marking grammatical boundaries within sentences.

Independent work

- Children continue or complete their writing.

Plenary

- Provide feedback and encouragement to the children in their writing.

DAY 5

Big Book pp. 35–39; Pupil's Book p. 90

Shared reading

- Compare the two extracts. Which do the children like best? Why? Compare the atmosphere in the two, and the use of language which creates it.
- In what ways are the two stories different?
- Ask the children to read aloud the story on pages 38–39 of the Big Book, with a narrator and others reading the dialogue.

Focused word/sentence work

- Notice that the dialogue consists of only the spoken words. With one exception, we are not told the names of the speakers. Does this matter? What is the exception? Who is speaking then?
- Investigate compound words in the text: *leftover, overgrown, driveway*. Can the children suggest other compound words built from *over*? Discuss the difference in meaning of words such as *overtake* and *takeover*. Explain how knowing which words are used to build compound words can help with the spelling.
- Revise the use of the apostrophe in shortened forms in preparation for the independent work.

Independent work

- Page 90 in the Pupil's Book focuses on the apostrophe in shortened forms.

Plenary

- Review the week's work, re-emphasising teaching points.

Consolidation and extension

- Make a wall display of the children's stories with suitable illustrations and a large picture of a genie and the lamp.
- Encourage the children to read their stories aloud.
- Ask the children to write a letter in the role of Toby to a friend telling about the genie.

Homework

- Page 29 in the Homework Book gives further practice in building compound words and using them in sentences.

Unit 29 Word Puzzles

Key Learning Objectives

TL6 To compare forms or types of humour

TL7 To select, prepare, read aloud and recite by heart poetry that plays with language or entertains; to recognise rhyme, alliteration and other patterns of sound that create effects

TL15 To write poetry that uses sound to create effects

WL9 To recognise and spell the prefixes *ex-* and *mis-*

WL10 To use their knowledge of these prefixes to generate new words from root words, and to understand how they give clues to meaning

WL14 To explore homonyms which have the same spelling but multiple meanings

Range:	Poetry that plays with language, word puzzles, puns, riddles
Texts:	*Wild Flowers*, Peter Newell; *Riddle*, Judith Nicholls; Traditional riddles; *Strange but True*, Anon; *UR 2 GOOD*, Michael Rosen
Resources:	Big Book 3C pp. 40–43 Pupil's Book 3 pp. 91–93 Homework Book 3 p. 30: New words from old – prefixes: *mis-*, *ex-* Copymaster 27: Collecting types of humour

Preparation

- Make dictionaries available throughout the week, preferably *Collins Primary Dictionary* or *Collins Independent Dictionary*.

DAY 1
Big Book pp. 40–42; Pupil's Book p. 92

Shared reading

- Read, discuss, enjoy and explain the riddles in this unit. Clues are given in the artwork. The answers are in question 1 of *To think and talk about* on page 42 of the Big Book. The two question riddles rely on the different meanings of the homonyms *tongue* and *calf*. Explain that such a play on words is called a pun.
- Read the verse *Wild Flowers*. The point of this lies in the pun on the word *wild*. What similarity does this verse have to the first two riddles?
- Discuss why the Thomas a Tattamus riddle is a tongue-twister.

Focused word/sentence work

- Use a dictionary to explore homonyms, e.g. *counter*, *cross*, *fast*, *fly*, *peak*. Ask the children to make up sentences to show the different meanings.
- Make up punning riddles from them, e.g. Why was the top of the mountain busy? Because it was peak time.

Independent work

- Children answer questions on the word puzzles.

Plenary

- Review the children's independent work.

DAY 2
Big Book p. 42; Pupil's Book p. 92

Shared reading

- Read the puzzle poem *Strange but True*. Challenge the children to explain how the poem can possibly be true. If the class cannot work it out for themselves, explain that the true meaning of the puzzle is revealed if a comma is placed after *fishpond* and then after the noun in the middle of each line after that.

Focused word/sentence work

- Remind the children of the importance of commas in marking the grammatical boundaries in sentences.
- Revise homonyms. Ask the children to look for examples in the dictionary, e.g. *miss*, *well*, *mark*. Encourage the children to use them in sentences to show their different meanings.
- Prepare for the independent work on page 92 in the Pupil's Book by making sure the children know how to complete a crossword.

Independent work

- Children explore homonyms and complete a crossword. Make a dictionary available for this activity.

Plenary

- Review the children's work on homonyms.

DAY 3
Pupil's Book p. 93

Shared writing, including focused word work

- Discuss possible clues for the completed crossword on page 93 in the Pupil's Book.
- Explore ways of making riddles using two meanings of homonyms.
- Encourage the children to make up their own riddles based on puns with homonyms.

Independent work

- Children write their own crossword clues and riddles.

Plenary

- Encourage the children to test out their riddles on the rest of the class.

DAY 4

Big Book p. 43; Pupil's Book p. 93

Shared reading/writing, including focused word work

- Read the poems on page 43 in the Big Book.
- Ask the children to explain Michael Rosen's play on words and numbers.
- Discuss the clues in Judith Nicholls's kangaroo poem. Use it as a model to write a riddle poem for another animal, e.g. an elephant.

Independent work

- Children write their own riddle poem, using Judith Nicholls's poem as a model.

Plenary

- Ask the children to read their work aloud.

DAY 5

Big Book pp. 40–43; Pupil's Book p. 93

Shared reading

- Read again the riddles and poems in this unit. Ask the children to compare them, and classify them into their different forms or types of humour.
- Copymaster 27 will help with this activity.
- Look back at the poems in Unit 22 and compare and classify those too.
- Discuss which poems the children like best and why.

Focused word/sentence work

- Look for words in the dictionary which have several meanings. Investigate how these are sometimes different parts of speech, e.g. *show* as a noun and as a verb. *Collins Independent Dictionary* identifies parts of speech.
- Use dictionaries to explore words which begin with the prefixes *ex-* and *mis-*.
- Explain how to find the homonym which links the two meanings given on page 93 in the Pupil's Book.
- Discuss how to write a tongue-twister, using alliteration. These work best when words with two very similar sounds are placed frequently together, e.g. "Peter Piper picked a peck of pickled pepper", where *pick* and *peck* tend to trip up the tongue.

Independent work

- Children work on homonyms and tongue-twisters.

Plenary

- Discuss the clues in the homonym puzzle. How many other meanings can the children think of for these words? Encourage the children to use the definitions to make up punning riddles, e.g. Why is a clever boy like a needle? Because he is sharp.

Consolidation and extension

- Ask the children to read aloud their favourite poems in this unit.
- Encourage the children to test out their tongue-twisters and riddles on the rest of the class.
- Create a class collection of riddles using as models those with which the children are familiar.
- Copymaster 27 encourages the children to collect riddles and poems and to classify them into their different forms or types of humour.

Homework

- Page 30 in the Homework Book investigates using the prefixes *mis-* and *ex-*.

Unit 30 Letters

Key Learning Objectives

TL16 To read examples of letters written for a range of purposes

TL20 To write letters, notes and messages, selecting style and vocabulary appropriate to the intended reader

TL23 To organise letters into simple paragraphs

WL16 To collect, investigate, classify common expressions from reading and own experience

Range:	Letters written for a range of purposes
Texts:	Letters
	From *Fred and the Angel* by Martin Waddell (on Copymaster 28)
Resources:	Big Book 3C pp. 44–48
	Pupil's Book 3 pp. 94–96
	Homework Book 3 p. 31: Proofreading
	Homework Book 3 p. 32: Revision
	Copymaster 28: Collecting common expressions
	Copymaster 29: Self-assessment sheet
	Copymaster 30: Assessment master for term 3

Preparation

- Make available suitable informal and formal letters and envelopes for exploring layouts: greetings, endings, paragraphs, addresses, etc.
- Writing activities are planned to take place on days 3, 4 and 5.

DAY 1
Big Book pp. 44–48; Pupil's Book p. 95

Shared reading

- Read the different kinds of letters on pages 44–48 of the Big Book. Investigate their form and layout. Look at the different ways of starting and ending. Which letters are informal, and which formal? Ask the children to justify their answers. Look at the different ways formal and informal letters begin and end.
- Reread each letter in turn. Identify the purpose and audience. Investigate how the form and style of the letter is influenced by purpose and audience.

Focused word/sentence work

- Collect ways of opening and ending letters, relating them to purpose and audience.

Independent work

- Children answer questions about the letters.

Plenary

- Review the children's independent work.

DAY 2
Big Book pp. 44–48; Pupil's Book p. 95

Shared reading/writing, including focused word/sentence work

- Read the letters on pages 44–48 of the Big Book.
- Which person is each letter written in? Which is the informal letter? Ask the children to justify their answers.
- Classify all the letters in this unit as letters to relate, enquire, comment, congratulate, complain, etc.

Independent work

- Page 95 in the Pupil's Book focuses on transforming first, second and third person accounts.

Plenary

- Review the children's work on the first, second and third person.

DAY 3
Pupil's Book p. 96

Shared reading/writing, including focused word/sentence work

- Select one of the letter-writing suggestions on page 96 in the Pupil's Book. Ask the children to identify the purpose of the letter. Who is to be written for? What style should it use: formal or informal? What would make a suitable greeting and ending?
- Plan the letter in paragraphs.
- Show the children how the letter should be set out.

Independent work

- Children plan and write their own letter, identifying purpose, audience and style.

Plenary

- Review the children's writing and understanding of purpose, audience and style.

DAY 4
Big Book pp. 44–48; Pupil's Book p. 96

Shared reading/writing

- Read a selection of different kinds of letter, using examples from the Big Book, the children's own writing and any you have collected.
- Discuss similarities and differences in purpose, style and audience.
- Make a list of greetings and endings, matching them to purpose and audience.
- Select another writing suggestion from page 96 of the Pupil's Book, but reserving the letter to an author for day 5.
- Plan and write the letter together.

Focused word/sentence work

- Discuss common ways of greeting in everyday speech.
- Discuss expressions for thanking, refusing, warning, expressing surprise, apology, etc.
- Copymaster 28 is a useful sheet for identifying and collecting such expressions.

Independent work

- Children write the letter planned together earlier in the lesson.

Plenary

- Discuss the children's writing, offering help and encouragement.

DAY 5
Pupil's Book p. 96

Shared writing

- Ask the children to choose an author whose books they have enjoyed. What would like to say to him or her, and what would they like to ask?
- Discuss purpose, audience and style when writing to an author.
- Plan the content of the letter, using the suggestions on page 96 in the Pupil's Book. Ask the children to suggest how it might be organised into paragraphs.

Focused word/sentence work

- Discuss proofreading. Why is it more important to have a fully correct formal letter than an informal one?

Independent work

- Children write their own letter to an author.

Plenary

- Review the week's work, re-emphasising teaching points.

Consolidation and extension

- Ask the children to read aloud some of their letters. Re-emphasise purpose, audience and style.
- Copymaster 28 is a useful sheet for identifying and collecting expressions for thanking, refusing, warning, expressing surprise, apology, etc.
- Copymaster 29 is a self-assessment sheet for the children to record the aspects of language they enjoy or find easy, and those they would like more help with. The completed sheet will be useful to the children's next teacher.
- At the end of the Copymasters section is a certificate for special achievement in any aspect of English, to be awarded at the teacher's discretion.

Homework

- Page 31 in the Homework Book focuses on proofreading: spelling, punctuation and speech marks.
- Page 32 in the Homework Book tests the children's understanding of the past tense of verbs, and the use of personal pronouns and adjectives.

ASSESSMENT

Copymaster 30 is an assessment master of key word and sentence objectives for term 3, testing use of conjunctions, homonyms, pronouns, sentence construction and punctuation. Indirectly, it will also test vocabulary, spelling and handwriting. The completed sheet will be useful as a record of progress, together with examples of the pupil's text work.

Copymasters

Name _____

Copymaster 1 Unit 1

Collecting story openings

Does the first sentence of a story make you want to read on? Use this sheet to collect the interesting openings of stories you enjoy.

Story	**Opening sentence**
The Moving Mystery	Rat-tat-tat!

Focus on Literacy Teacher's Resource Book 3 © Barry and Anita Scholes, HarperCollins*Publishers* Ltd 1999

Copymaster 2 Unit 1

Look, say, cover, write, check

The secret of better Spelling

Look

Say

Cover

Write

Check

Use **Look, say, cover, write, check** to learn these words.

Look, say, cover	Write	Check	Try again	Check
jump	jump	✓		
home				
house				
door				
ball				

Focus on Literacy Teacher's Resource Book 3 © Barry and Anita Scholes, HarperCollins*Publishers* Ltd 1999

87

Copymaster 3
Unit 1

Name _____

Words I know

Use this sheet to write the words you know how to spell.

a	b	c	d	e
f	g	h	i	j
k	l	m	n	o
p	q	r	s	t
u	v	w	x	y	z

Name _____

**Copymaster 4
Unit 3**

Characters: cutouts for stick puppets

Colour and cut out these characters from the play "The School Bell". Make them into stick puppets for presenting your playscript to an audience.

Story-teller

Miss Cross

Ali

Kate

Grant

Mrs Sorter

Focus on Literacy Teacher's Resource Book 3 © Barry and Anita Scholes, HarperCollins*Publishers* Ltd 1999

89

**Copymaster 5
Unit 4**

Collecting verbs

Collect these different kinds of verbs from your reading.

Verbs for speaking loudly

Verbs for speaking softly

Other verbs for speaking

Verbs for animal sounds (give the animal's name)

Copymaster 6 Unit 5

A home for a pet

Name _____

A home for a _____

Name _____

Copymaster 7 Unit 6

The senses

Name _____

Copymaster 8
Unit 8

The Flat Man

Focus on Literacy Teacher's Resource Book 3 © Barry and Anita Scholes, HarperCollins*Publishers* Ltd 1999

Name _____

Collecting new words

Collecting new words from your reading helps you learn what they mean and how they are spelled.

Collect words on these subjects, and write their meanings in the appropriate boxes.

Write the name of your hobby or interest, and use the fourth box for a subject of your choice.

Science words

Words about birds

Migrate: to move at a particular season to a different place

Words about _____

Words about my hobby: _____

Copymaster 9
Unit 9

94

Focus on Literacy Teacher's Resource Book 3 © Barry and Anita Scholes, HarperCollins*Publishers* Ltd 1999

Copymaster 10 Unit 10

Revision

1. Answer these questions in complete sentences:

   a) Where do you live?

   b) Who are your best friends?

   c) What did you do yesterday?

   _____
   _____
   _____

2. Write two sentences: one a question, the other an exclamation.

   _____
   _____

3. Complete these sentences.

   a) Mum said, "_____

   b) "Help!" _____

4. Make a new word from each of these words, using each prefix only once. Use each word in a sentence to show its meaning.

   | mist appear build tend tidy   dis- un- pre- de- re- |

   _____
   _____
   _____
   _____

Focus on Literacy Teacher's Resource Book 3 © Barry and Anita Scholes, HarperCollinsPublishers Ltd 1999

Name _____

Storyboard

Title _____

1	2	3

Notes/word bank

4	5	6

Notes/word bank

Copymaster 11
Unit 11

Name _____

Fiction book review

Title _____

Author _____

Reviewed by _____

Where does the story take place? _____

Who is the story about? _____

What kind of person is he/she? _____

What does this character do in the story? _____

If you met him/her what would you like to say? _____

Copymaster 12
Unit 11

Focus on Literacy Teacher's Resource Book 3 © Barry and Anita Scholes, HarperCollins*Publishers* Ltd 1999

Copymaster 13
Unit 12

Name _____

Writing a letter

Your address _____

_____

_____

The name of the person you are writing to

Your postcode _____

Date _____

_____

Sign off with *Yours sincerely*, or if you are writing to a close friend or relative you might write *Love from*.

_____

Sign your name _____

Copymaster 14
Unit 13

Name _____

Planning a story

Use this sheet to help you plan a story.

Characters (Who is your story about?)
_____
_____
_____

Setting (Where does your story take place?)
_____

Paragraph 1: the beginning (How does your story begin?)
_____
_____
_____
_____

Paragraph 2: the middle (What happens in the middle?)
_____
_____
_____
_____

Paragraph 3: the ending (How does it end?)
_____
_____
_____
_____

The opening sentence The first sentence of your story is very important. Write your idea for an interesting opening sentence here.
_____

Focus on Literacy Teacher's Resource Book 3 © Barry and Anita Scholes, HarperCollins*Publishers* Ltd 1999

Name _____

**Copymaster 15
Unit 13**

Book review: a story

Title _____

Author _____

Who is the story about? _____
_____

Where does the story take place? _____
_____

What is the opening sentence? _____
_____

What happens at the beginning of the story?
_____
_____
_____
_____

What happens in the middle of the story?
_____
_____
_____
_____

How does the story end?
_____
_____
_____
_____

Focus on Literacy Teacher's Resource Book 3 © Barry and Anita Scholes, HarperCollins*Publishers* Ltd 1999

Copymaster 16
Unit 15

Making notes

The key words are the most important words in a text. Without them the text will not make sense.

Short unimportant words such as **a** and **the** can usually be left out without affecting the sense.

Look at this instruction:

Mix coconut and **sugar** with the **milk. If coconut** is **very dry, use less** than the quantity given, **or sweets may go hard**.

The key words may then be written as notes:

Mix coconut, sugar, milk. If coconut very dry, use less or sweets may go hard.

Highlight the key words in these instructions. Then rewrite them as notes.

Vanishing Colours

1. Cut out a disc from the card.
2. Divide it into six equal parts, using a protractor. Each segment should have an angle of 60 degrees.
3. Colour the segments in the order colours appear in the rainbow: red, orange, yellow, green, blue and violet.
4. Make a hole in the centre of the disc and carefully push the dowling through so that it is fairly tight.
5. Hold the dowling between your hands with the colours facing up. Rub your hands back and forth to spin the disc and watch what happens.

Notes:

Copymaster 17
Unit 15

A recipe

Name _____

Write a recipe for one of your favourite dishes. Use the headings below to help you.

Recipe for _____

Ingredients

Equipment

Method

1.

2.

3.

4.

Read through your recipe.
Have you missed anything out?
Is everything in the right order?

Copymaster 18
Unit 16

Achi and Nine Men's Morris

These are the boards for the games of Achi and Nine Men's Morris. You may prefer to enlarge these to A3 when copying.

Achi

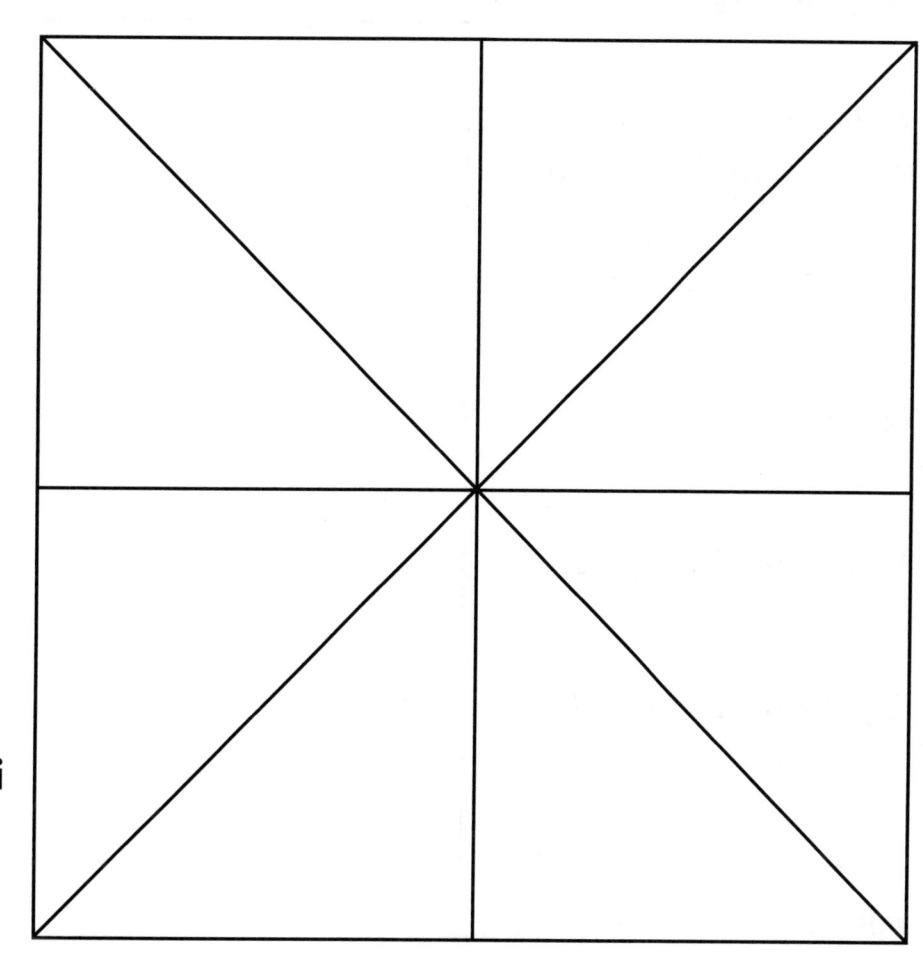

Nine Men's Morris

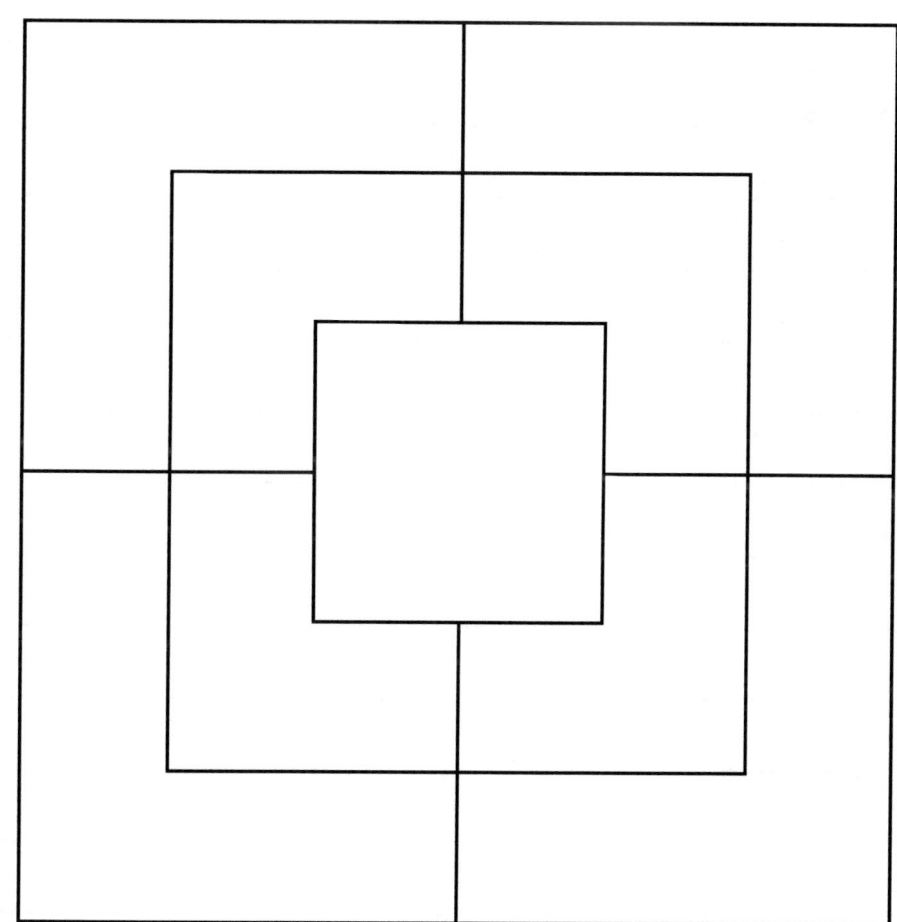

Focus on Literacy Teacher's Resource Book 3 © Barry and Anita Scholes, HarperCollins*Publishers* Ltd 1999

Copymaster 19
Unit 16

Name _____

Rules for a board game

Write your own directions for any board game you know well.
Draw the playing board.

Name of game
_____

Number of players:
_____

Equipment needed:
_____
_____

Aim of the game: _____
_____

Playing board

Rules: _____
_____
_____
_____
_____
_____
_____
_____
_____
_____

104

Focus on Literacy Teacher's Resource Book 3 © Barry and Anita Scholes, HarperCollins*Publishers* Ltd 1999

**Copymaster 20
Unit 20**

Revision

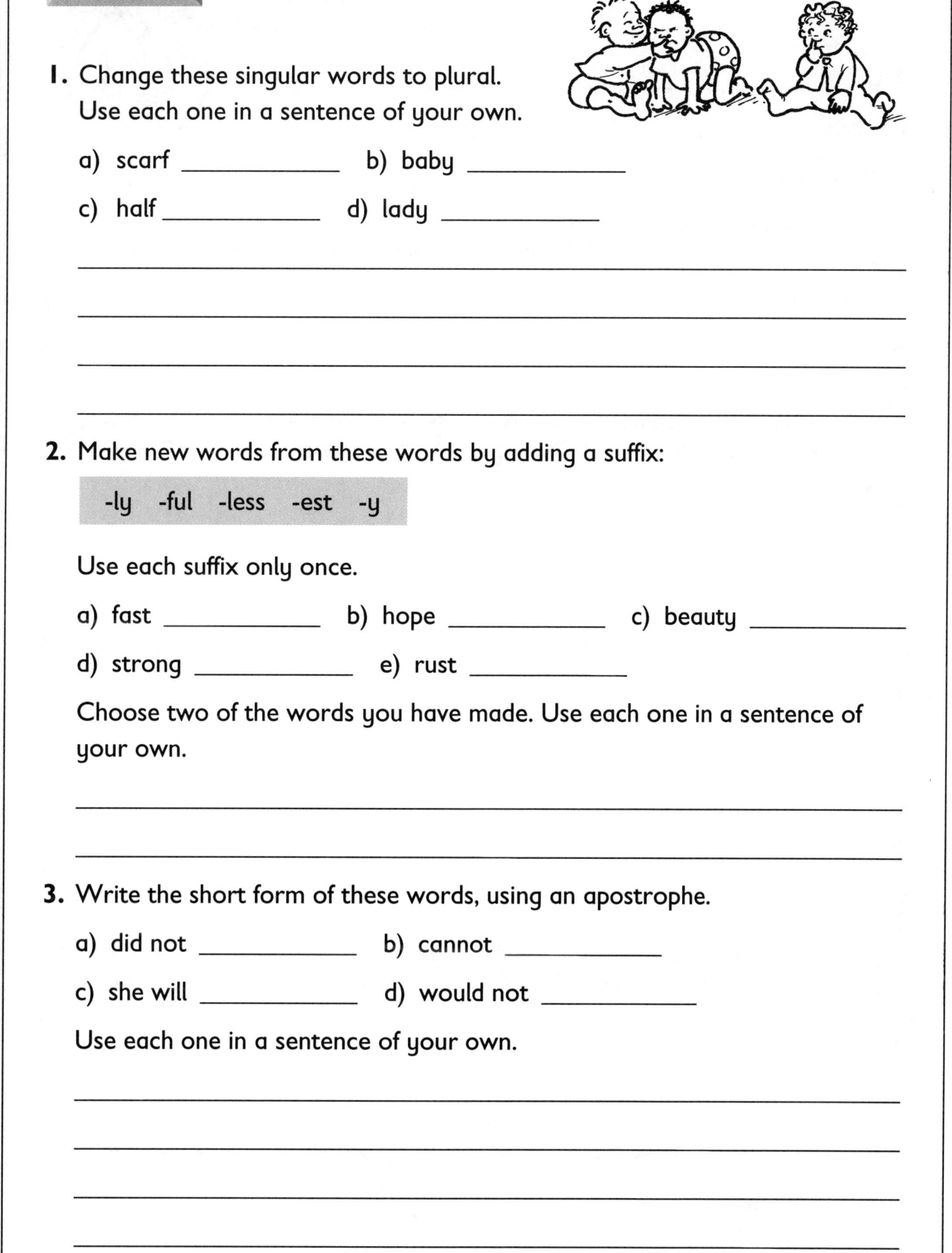

1. Change these singular words to plural.
   Use each one in a sentence of your own.

   a) scarf _____ b) baby _____

   c) half _____ d) lady _____

   _____

   _____

   _____

2. Make new words from these words by adding a suffix:

   -ly   -ful   -less   -est   -y

   Use each suffix only once.

   a) fast _____ b) hope _____ c) beauty _____

   d) strong _____ e) rust _____

   Choose two of the words you have made. Use each one in a sentence of your own.

   _____

   _____

3. Write the short form of these words, using an apostrophe.

   a) did not _____ b) cannot _____

   c) she will _____ d) would not _____

   Use each one in a sentence of your own.

   _____

   _____

   _____

   _____

Focus on Literacy Teacher's Resource Book 3 © Barry and Anita Scholes, HarperCollins*Publishers* Ltd 1999

Copymaster 21
Unit 23

Book review

Brilliant!

Title _____

Author _____

Main characters _____

Tell the story in your own words.

Beginning

Middle

End

What is the main idea of the book? _____

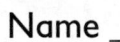

Book review

Title _____

Author _____

An exciting incident

Describe in your own words an exciting incident from the book.

_____
_____
_____
_____

Select words or phrases from the book which make that incident exciting.

[ ]

Do you think this incident could have really happened? Give a reason for your answer.

_____
_____

Main character

How did the main character feel at that time?

_____
_____

Why did he or she behave in that way?

_____
_____

What do you think about the way that character reacted?

_____
_____

Name _____

**Copymaster 23
Unit 24**

Finding out about Roald Dahl

Look at the covers of books by Roald Dahl, and other sources, to find out about his life.

Date and place of birth

Date he died

Early life

Later life

Books by Roald Dahl

A Roald Dahl book I have read and why I like it

Focus on Literacy Teacher's Resource Book 3 © Barry and Anita Scholes, HarperCollins*Publishers* Ltd 1999

Name _____

Copymaster 24
Unit 24

Comparing books by the same author

Choose two books by the same author you have read and enjoyed. For each book, think about the setting, main character, plot (story) and theme (main idea). Write your ideas here.

Title		
Setting Where does the story take place?		
Main character What kind of person? What do you think about them?		
Plot What are the main events?		
Theme What is the main idea of the book?		

In what ways are the two books similar? In what ways are they different?
_____
_____

Which book do you prefer? Why? _____
_____
_____

Focus on Literacy Teacher's Resource Book 3 © Barry and Anita Scholes, HarperCollins*Publishers* Ltd 1999

Fiction books

Look in your class or school library for books by these authors. Write down their titles. Put a tick against those you have read.

Title	Title
Dick King-Smith	
Jacqueline Wilson	
Lisa Bruce	
Hazel Townson	
Shirley Hughes	
Terry Jones	
David McKee	
Anthony Browne	
Margaret Mahy	
Bob Wilson	
Grace Hallworth	
Roald Dahl	
Chris Powling	
Anne Fine	
Allan Ahlberg	

Non-fiction books

Look in your class or school library for books on these subjects. You may use sub-topics. Write down the titles.

Title	Title
Food _____	_____
Trees _____	_____
Insects _____	_____
Famous people _____	_____
Music _____	_____
Sport _____	_____
Magnetism _____	_____
Space travel _____	_____
Ships _____	_____
The Romans _____	_____
Australia _____	_____
Buildings _____	_____
Mathematics _____	_____
Computers _____	_____
Water _____	_____

Copymaster 27
Unit 29

Name _____

Collecting types of humour

Use this sheet to collect the titles of different types of humour: poems, riddles, etc.

Word play

Joke poems

Word games

Absurdities

Cautionary tales

Nonsense verse

Calligrams

112

Focus on Literacy Teacher's Resource Book 3 © Barry and Anita Scholes, HarperCollins*Publishers* Ltd 1999

Collecting common expressions

Copymaster 28
Unit 30

Read this passage and underline the common expressions for surprise, congratulations, apology, warning, etc. Then copy the underlined expressions into the correct box below. You will not have an expression for every box.

Fred wanted to be an angel. One day Wortsley, the Chief Inspector of Angels, called Fred to his cloud.

"Congratulations, Fred!" Wortsley said. "You have passed your Angel Exams!"

"Yippee!" cried Fred, throwing his harp up in the air. It went a long way up and hit a passing Saint on the ear.

"Ouch!" said the Saint. "Who threw that harp?"

"Oh, gosh!" said Fred. "I"m terribly sorry. It was me!"

"I forgive you," said the Saint. Saints are like that.

"Not a good start, Fred," said Wortsley, with a frown.

"I promise it won't happen again," said Fred.

From *Fred and the Angel* by Martin Waddell

Surprise	Apology	Greeting	Warning

Thanking	Refusing	Promising	Congratulating

Add to the boxes further examples of common expressions that you already know or find in your reading.

Focus on Literacy Teacher's Resource Book 3 © Barry and Anita Scholes, HarperCollins*Publishers* Ltd 1999

113

Name _____

Copymaster 29 Unit 30

How am I getting on?

Draw a smiling face next to the things you enjoy or find easy. ☺

Tick the things you would like more help with. ✓

Speaking, talking and listening

talking about stories or poems

reading aloud by myself

reading aloud with others

Writing

stories

playscripts

poems

letters

book reviews

reports

instructions

giving information

making notes

punctuation

spelling

Reading

story books

poems

plays

information books

using a contents page and index

using a dictionary

using a thesaurus

instructions

letters

114

Focus on Literacy Teacher's Resource Book 3 © Barry and Anita Scholes, HarperCollins*Publishers* Ltd 1999

Copymaster 30
Unit 30

Revision

1. Join these sentences with a suitable conjunction from the word bank. Use each conjunction only once.

   if   so   while   though   since   when

   a) It rained hard. He got wet.
   b) He lost the race. He ran very fast.
   c) I'll help you. I have the time.
   d) She'll have her tea. She gets home.
   e) You tidy up. I do the dusting.
   f) You will be late. You don't hurry.

2. Use each of these homonyms in two sentences of your own to show two different meanings:

   stamp   post

3. Use each pronoun in a sentence of your own:

   they   us   mine   theirs

115

Focus on Literacy Teacher's Resource Book 3 © Barry and Anita Scholes, HarperCollins*Publishers* Ltd 1999

Focus on Literacy 3
Achievement Award

Awarded to _____

For _____

Signed _____ Date _____

School _____

Focus on Literacy 3
Achievement Award

Awarded to _____

For _____

Signed _____ Date _____

School _____

Focus on Literacy Teacher's Resource Book 3 © Barry and Anita Scholes, HarperCollins*Publishers* Ltd 1999

RECORD SHEET

NAME _____   CLASS _____

Year 3 • Term 1

Word level work: phonics, spelling, vocabulary

Objective	Comment
Revision and consolidation from KS1	
1 Long vowel phonemes	
2 Phonemes: identify, blend, segment	
3 High frequency words	
4 Syllables	
Spelling strategies	
5 Identifying misspelt words	
6 Independent spelling strategies	
7 Look, say, cover, write, check	
Spelling conventions and rules	
8 -ing	
9 -le	
10 un-, dis, de-, re-, pre-	
11 New words from root words	
12 Using the term "prefix"	
Vocabulary extension	
13 Collecting new words	
14 Inference from context	
15 Dictionary	
16 Thesaurus	
17 Synonyms	
18 Using the term "synonym"	
19 Vocabulary for introducing and concluding dialogue	
Handwriting	
20 Formation of basic joins	
21 Consistency in size, proportion and spacing	

Sentence level work: grammar and punctuation

Objective	Comment
Grammatical awareness	
1 Deciphering new words	
2 Grammar and punctuation when reading aloud	
3 Function of verbs in sentences	
4 Verb tenses	
5 Using the term "verb"	
Sentence construction and punctuation	
6 Question marks and exclamation marks	
7 Speech punctuation	
8 Using the term "speech marks"	
9 Other ways of presenting text	

Focus on Literacy Teacher's Resource Book 3 © Barry and Anita Scholes, HarperCollins*Publishers* Ltd 1999

YEAR 3 TERM 1 RECORD SHEET

Sentence level work: grammar and punctuation *continued*

Objective	Comment
Revision and consolidation from KS1	
10 Boundaries between separate sentences	
11 Writing in complete sentences	
12 Full stops and capital letters	
13 Commas in a list	

Text level work: comprehension and composition

Objective	Comment
Fiction and poetry	
Reading comprehension	
1 Setting	
2 Dialogue	
3 Different voices used in stories	
4 Playscripts	
5 Key differences between prose and playscript	
6 Read aloud and recite poems	
7 Distinguishing between rhyming and non-rhyming poetry	
8 Express views	
Writing composition	
9 Generating ideas	
10 Writing own passages of dialogue	
11 Writing short description of a known place	
12 Collecting words and phrases to write poems and short descriptions	
13 Writing calligrams and shape poems	
14 Writing simple playscripts	
15 Organising stories into paragraphs	
Non-fiction	
Reading comprehension	
16 Distinguishing between fact and fiction	
17 Noticing differences in the style and structure of fiction and non-fiction writing	
18 Using contents	
19 Comparing presentation of information	
20 Identifying main points in information text	
Writing composition	
21 Recording information	
22 Simple non-chronological writing	

RECORD SHEET

NAME _____ CLASS _____

Year 3 • Term 2

Word level work: phonics, spelling, vocabulary

Objective	Comment
Revision and consolidation from KS1	
1 Long vowel phonemes	
2 Phonemes: identify, blend, segment	
3 High frequency words	
4 Syllables	
Spelling strategies	
5 Identifying misspelt words	
6 Independent spelling strategies	
7 Look, say, cover, write, check	
Spelling conventions and rules	
8 -er, -est, -y	
9 Spelling of nouns when -s is added	
10 Silent letters	
11 Using the terms "singular" and "plural"	
12 Compound words	
13 Common suffixes	
14 New words from root words	
15 Apostrophe in shortened forms	
16 Uusing the term "suffix"	
Vocabulary extension	
17 Collecting new words	
18 Inferring meaning from context	
19 Using dictionaries for spellings and definitions	
20 Own definitions	
21 Using the term "definition"	
22 Quartiles of the dictionary	
23 Alphabetical order, to second letters	
24 Opposites	
Handwriting	
25 Formation of basic joins	
26 Consistency in size, proportion and spacing	
27 Speed, fluency, legibility	

Focus on Literacy Teacher's Resource Book 3 © Barry and Anita Scholes, HarperCollins*Publishers* Ltd 1999

YEAR 3 TERM 2 RECORD SHEET

Sentence level work: grammar and punctuation

Objective	Comment
Grammatical awareness	
1 Deciphering new words	
2 Adjectives	
3 Using the term "adjective"	
4 Plurals	
5 Using the terms "singular" and "plural"	
Sentence construction and punctuation	
6 Commas	
7 Using the term "comma"	
8 Capitalisation	
9 Words essential to meaning and which not	
10 Verbs in 1st, 2nd and 3rd person	
11 Need for grammatical agreement	

Text level work: comprehension and composition

Objective	Comment
Fiction and poetry	
Reading comprehension	
1 Traditional story language	
2 Story themes	
3 Recurring characters	
4 Performing poems	
5 Rehearsing and improving performance	
Writing composition	
6 Plannning main points in story writing	
7 Describing and sequencing key incidents	
8 Characters' portraits	
9 Story plan for own myth, fable, traditional tale	
10 Sequels to traditional stories	
11 Writing new or extended verses for performance	
Non-fiction	
Reading comprehension	
12 Purposes of instructional texts	
13 Merits and limitations of particular instructional texts	
14 How instructions are organised	
15 Reading and following simple instructions	
Writing composition	
16 Writing instructions	
17 Making clear notes	

RECORD SHEET

NAME _____ CLASS _____

Year 3 • Term 3

Word level work: phonics, spelling, vocabulary

Objective	Comment
Revision and consolidation from KS1	
1 Long vowel phonemes	
2 Phonemes: identify, blend, segment	
3 High frequency words	
4 Syllables	
Spelling strategies	
5 Identifying misspelt words	
6 Independent spelling strategies	
7 Look, say, cover, write, check	
Spelling conventions and rules	
8 Short words within longer words	
9 *mis-, non-, co-, anti-*	
10 Use prefixes to generate new words from root words	
11 Apostrophe in contracted forms	
12 Collecting new words	
13 Synonyms useful in writing dialogue	
14 Homonyms	
15 Dictionaries: further information about words	
16 Common expressions	
Handwriting	
17 Formation of basic joins	
18 Consistency in size, proportion and spacing	
19 Speed, fluency, legibility	

Sentence level work: grammar and punctuation

Objective	Comment
Grammatical awareness	
1 Deciphering new words	
2 Pronouns	
3 Grammatical agreement of pronouns and verbs	
Sentence construction and punctuation	
4 Speech marks and other dialogue punctuation	
5 Joining sentences: *if, so, while, though, since, when*	
6 Words and phrases which signal time sequences	
7 Commas marking grammatical boundaries within sentences	

Focus on Literacy Teacher's Resource Book 3 © Barry and Anita Scholes, HarperCollins*Publishers* Ltd 1999

Text level work: comprehension and composition

Objective	Comment
Fiction and poetry	
Reading comprehension	
1 Story sequence; comparing, evaluating, justifying preference	
2 Referring to significant aspects of text	
3 Distinguishing between 1st and 3rd person accounts	
4 Considering credibility of events	
5 Characters' feelings, behaviour and relationships	
6 Comparing forms or types of humour	
7 Read aloud poetry	
8 Comparing works by same author	
9 Awareness of authors	
Writing composition	
10 Plotting sequence of episodes modelled on known story	
11 Writing linked to or arising from reading stories	
12 Writing a 1st person account	
13 Writing more extended stories	
14 Book reviews	
15 Writing poetry that uses sound to create effects	
Non-fiction	
Reading comprehension	
16 Letters	
17 Scanning for information	
18 Locating books by classification	
19 Summarising orally	
Writing composition	
20 Writing letters, notes, messages	
21 Using IT	
22 Recounting in a variety of ways	
23 Organising letters in paragraphs	
24 Making alphabetically ordered texts	
25 Note-making	
26 Summarising in writing	

Appendices

NLS and *Focus on Literacy*: overview charts

Term 1

Word level	Sentence level	Text level
1 Continuous work	1 Continuous work	1 Units 1, 2, 4, 8
2 Continuous work	2 Units 1, 2, 3, 4	2 Units 1, 2, 3, 4, 5
3 Continuous work	3 Units 4, 5	3 Units 1, 2, 4
4 Continuous work	4 Units 5, 8	4 Unit 3
5 Continuous work	5 Units 4, 5	5 Units 3, 4
6 Continuous work; Unit 7	6 Units 1, 3	6 Units 6, 10
7 Continuous work	7 Units 2, 4	7 Units 6, 10
8 Units 2, 8	8 Unit 4	8 Units 1, 2, 4, 5, 6, 8, 10
9 Unit 2	9	9 Continuous work; Units 2, 6, 7, 9
10 Units 4, 8	10 Continuous work	10 Unit 4
11 Units 4, 8	11 Continuous work; Units 1, 2	11 Unit 8
12 Units 4, 8	12 Continuous work; Unit 1	12 Units 6, 10
13 Continuous work; Unit 9	13 Continuous work; Units 1, 9	13 Unit 10
14 Unit 9		14 Unit 3
15 Unit 9		15 Unit 8
16 Units 6, 10		16 Unit 5
17 Unit 6		17 Units 5, 7, 8, 9
18 Unit 6		18 Unit 7
19 Unit 4		19 Units 7, 9
20 Continuous work		20 Units 5, 7, 9
21 Continuous work		21 Unit 9
		22 Units 7, 9

Term 2

Word level	Sentence level	Text level
1 Continuous work	1 Continuous work; Unit 19	1 Units 11, 12, 14, 18, 19, 20
2 Continuous work	2 Units 11, 14	2 Units 11, 12, 14, 20
3 Continuous work	3 Unit 12	3 Units 11, 12, 13, 14
4 Continuous work	4 Units 11, 13, 19	4 Units 16, 18
5 Continuous work	5 Units 13, 19	5 Units 16, 18
6 Continuous work	6 Units 13, 16, 18	6 Units 11, 13, 14, 18, 20
7 Continuous work; Unit 17	7 Units 13, 16	7 Units 12, 13, 14, 18
8 Unit 11	8 Units 13, 16	8 Units 13, 20
9 Units 11, 13, 19	9 Units 14, 18, 20	9 Units 11, 13, 14, 18, 20
10 Units 11, 17	10 Units 15, 16, 18, 20	10 Units 13, 19, 20
11	11 Units 12, 20	11 Unit 16
12		12 Units 15, 16
13 Unit 19		13 Units 15, 16
14 Unit 19		14 Units 15, 16
15 Unit 13		15 Units 15, 16
16 Unit 11		16 Units 15, 16
17 Continuous work		17 Units 15, 16
18 Unit 18		
19 Units 17, 18		
20 Unit 17		
21 Unit 17		
22 Unit 17		
23 Unit 17		
24 Unit 18		
25 Continuous work		
26 Continuous work		
27 Continuous work		

NLS AND *FOCUS ON LITERACY*: OVERVIEW CHARTS

Term 3

Word level	Sentence level	Text level
1 Continuous work	1 Continuous work	1 Units 23, 24, 25, 27, 28
2 Continuous work	2 Units 23, 25	2 Units 23, 24, 25, 27, 28
3 Continuous work	3 Unit 23	3 Units 23, 24, 25, 27, 28
4 Continuous work	4 Unit 24	4 Units 23, 24, 25, 27, 28
5 Continuous work	5 Units 24, 27	5 Units 23, 24, 25, 27, 28
6 Continuous work	6 Units 24, 28	6 Units 22, 29
7 Continuous work	7 Units 23, 24, 25, 28	7 Units 22, 29
8		8 Units 23, 24, 28
9 Units 22, 29		9 Units 23, 24, 28
10 Unit 29		10 Units 23, 27, 28
11 Unit 27		11 Units 23, 28
12 Continuous work		12 Units 23, 25, 27
13 Unit 25		13 Unit 24
14 Units 21, 25, 27, 29		14 Units 23, 24
15 Units 21, 25		15 Units 22, 29
16 Unit 30		16 Unit 30
17 Continuous work		17 Units 21, 26
18 Continuous work		18 Unit 26
19 Continuous work		19 Unit 26
		20 Unit 30
		21 Unit 26
		22 Unit 28
		23 Unit 30
		24 Units 21, 26
		25 Unit 26
		26 Unit 26

High frequency words to be taught through Year R to Year 2

These words should be revised during Year 3.

Reception

I	go	come	went
up	you	day	was
look	are	the	of
we	this	dog	me
like	going	big	she
and	they	my	see
on	away	mum	it
at	play	no	yes
for	a	dad	can
he	am	all	
is	cat	get	
said	to	in	

Years 1 to 2

about	had	night	three
after	half	not	time
again	has	now	too
an	have	off	took
another	help	old	tree
as	her	once	two
back	here	one	us
ball	him	or	very
be	his	our	want
because	home	out	water
bed	house	over	way
been	how	people	were
boy	if	push	what
brother	jump	pull	when
but	just	put	where
by	last	ran	who
call(ed)	laugh	saw	will
came	little	school	with
can't	live(d)	seen	would
could	love	should	your
did	made	sister	
do	make	so	**Plus:**
don't	man	some	• days of the week
dig	many	take	• months of the year
door	may	than	• numbers to twenty
down	more	that	• common colour words
first	much	their	• pupil's name and address
from	must	them	
girl	name	then	• name and address of school
good	new	there	
got	next	these	

127